Brenda Kunneman reminds us that it doesn't matter how much the devil has tampered with our past; God has a blueprint for our future. Gaining insight from master builder Nehemiah, Brenda shares practical and spiritual principles to help us get back on track and finish every work we start.

—JOY STRANG
CFO, STRANG COMMUNICATIONS COMPANY

Brenda Kunneman is a commanding voice as an anointed, prophetic teacher. Her book *When Your Life Has Been Tampered With* will unveil the one destroying your hopes and dreams, end the vicious cycle of destruction in your life, and open new doors to a brighter you. Get ready to be transformed!

—GUILLERMO MALDONADO
SENIOR PASTOR, EL REY JESÚS MINISTRIES
MIAMI, FLORIDA

There are many ministries but few places where people can get real *ministry*! When I meditate on the work that Brenda Kunneman and her husband, Hank, do for the Lord, I hear the words *real ministry*! God has graced Brenda to be an awesome gift to the body of Christ. She has prophetic insight, a warfare edge, and a burden for the brokenhearted. You cannot afford to keep her new book, *When Your Life Has Been Tampered With*, out of your library.

—KIMBERLY DANIELS
APOSTLE AND OVERSEER, KIMBERLY DANIELS MINISTRIES INTERNATIONAL
JACKSONVILLE, FLORIDA

Brenda is writing about a very raw nerve in the body of Christ. Her book presents a biblical solution and an anointing of power. I so appreciate her boldness and openness to help us open our own hearts.

—DR. MARILYN HICKEY
PRESIDENT, MARILYN HICKEY MINISTRIES
FOUNDING PASTOR, ORCHARD ROAD CHRISTIAN CENTER

I know Brenda Kunneman, and she is a woman who listens to the voice of God. She is a preacher and a prophet who has the gift to know how to communicate to other people what God wants to say. I have seen her not only communicating God's will to His people in general, but also speaking specific words to people, churches, and nations. I am sure that this book, *When Your Life Has Been Tampered With,* is a result of the time that Brenda has spent listening to God. Read it and get ready to rise up and fulfill the plans God designed for your life.

—Dr. Cash E. Luna
Pastor, Casa de Dios
Guatemala City, Guatemala

When Your
LIFE
HAS BEEN
Tampered
WITH

Brenda Kunneman

Charisma
HOUSE
A STRANG COMPANY

Most Strang Communications/Charisma House/Siloam/ Christian Life/FrontLine/Excel Books/Realms products are available at special quantity discounts for bulk purchase for sales promotions, premiums, fund-raising, and educational needs. For details, write Strang Communications/Charisma House/Siloam/Christian Life/ FrontLine/Excel Books/Realms, 600 Rinehart Road, Lake Mary, Florida 32746, or telephone (407) 333-0600.

When Your Life Has Been Tampered With
by Brenda Kunneman
Published by Charisma House
A Strang Company
600 Rinehart Road
Lake Mary, Florida 32746
www.charismahouse.com

Unless otherwise noted, all Scripture quotations are from the King James Version of the Bible.

Scripture quotations marked AMP are from The Amplified Bible. Old Testament copyright © 1965, 1987 by the Zondervan Corporation. The Amplified New Testament copyright © 1954, 1958, 1987 by the Lockman Foundation. Used by permission.

Scripture quotations marked NIV are from the Holy Bible, New International Version. Copyright © 1973, 1978, 1984, International Bible Society. Used by permission.

Scripture quotations marked NLT are from the Holy Bible, New Living Translation, copyright © 1996, 2004. Used by permission of Tyndale House Publishers, Inc., Wheaton, IL 60189. All rights reserved.

Design Director: Bill Johnson
Cover Designers: Amanda Potter, Bill Johnson, Karen Grindley

Library of Congress Cataloging-in-Publication Data:
Kunneman, Brenda.
  When your life has been tampered with / Brenda Kunneman.
      p. cm.
  ISBN 978-1-59979-280-4
  1. Spiritual warfare. 2. Christian life. I. Title.
  BV4509.5.K86 2008
  248.4--dc22

                                        2008007547

First Edition

08 09 10 11 12 — 9 8 7 6 5 4 3 2 1
Printed in the United States of America

This book is dedicated first to my husband, Hank, and our two sons, Matthew and Jonathan.

It is also dedicated to the church family of Lord of Hosts Church in Omaha, Nebraska, and the many people worldwide who have risen from difficult situations through God's love and power.

[CONTENTS]

1   Broken Dreams, Dust, and Ashes 1

2   Decide Your Season of Change. 29

3   Freedom From Captivity 55

4   The Enemies of the Mind. 79

5   This Cycle of Trouble Must Stop 105

6   The Eye of God Is Upon You. 131

7   Find and Rebuild Your God-given Purpose 155

8   The King's Decree Keeps Your Life on Course . . 183

9   The Anointing to Finish 209

[God said,] And I will put enmity between thee and the woman, and between thy seed and her seed; it shall bruise thy head, and thou shalt bruise his heel.

[GENESIS 3:15]

[CHAPTER 1]

BROKEN DREAMS, DUST, and ASHES

D*ECEIVED.* THAT WAS THE WORD THAT STUCK IN JEFF'S mind as he reflected on the events of his life. He had been living in his own world, and now he was lying in the hospital. How could all this be happening? Even though his parents divorced while he was very young, Jeff had been raised with Christian influence in his life. But nothing about him was turning out very Christian. He had a good job, paid his bills, and always tried to look his best, but more and more he found himself fitting in with a worldly lifestyle.

As a young adult, Jeff became comfortable hanging with his partying friends. He began doing drugs with them and also found himself as a regular patron of gay bars. Internally he was filled with rejection, shame, and fear. Something about this "Christian" young man was going terribly wrong.

It wasn't until he was stricken with pain—life-threatening pain—that he knew he was spiraling out of control. The medical report was that Jeff had several dangerous blood clots in his lungs. In the hospital, while waiting for his pain medicine and blood thinners, he called out to God. He even told the devil, "I don't care what you do to me, Satan, I know that Jesus died and rose again." Jeff believes that was the moment he received a real salvation experience extending beyond just head knowledge.

God spared Jeff's life from a serious medical condition, and after his hospital stay, Jeff began to go after the things of God. He started reading the Bible, listening to Christian radio, and trying to find a good church in the town where he lived.

There was one problem: privately, Jeff was in a prison of rejection. The captive lifestyle of his past was waiting to creep back in. He started smoking cigarettes again and slipping back into old habits. Jeff didn't want to live that way anymore, but he needed something to break the cycle in his life. After repeated failures he started to develop the idea that you could be a Christian, but you would probably struggle to live in any real victory until you get to heaven someday. He thought he would just have to tolerate a life of sin and repeated disappointment until Jesus came back. He was filled with guilt and shame from his past and, even as a Christian, struggled to find his purpose in God.

Then Jeff began attending a church that preached how you can live in the power of God in a very supernatural way, and a process began to take place. After listening to preaching filled with power, and hearing the prophetic word, he was able to set his face in a new direction—a direction toward God. Jeff began to realize that he *could* do something about the horrible demons and habits tampering with his life. Not only could he do it, he had to do it! This was his answer. Suddenly he began to rise up and take his life back.

After a little time, and simply for something to do one day, he tried to go back to the clubs. But something had happened; something had changed. For the first time, Jeff realized he couldn't be there in that place anymore. He had to leave. He had already left the place of captivity and was on the road to a new purpose. Jeff stood in the power of God and broke the chains of rejection, failure, and fear.

Deceived? Yes. Jeff had been tricked by the devil and was overcome by the circumstances in his own life.

My husband and I know Jeff and have watched him walk with God beautifully. We have seen how he finally realized that his life was repeatedly being tampered with, but he didn't have to live that way. We are thankful that our ministry has had a part in his life.

Jeff is not unlike many people who have struggled through things. For some it is addictions and bad habits; for others it's the pain of disappointment and tragedy. Still, many are just captive to their view of themselves, their income, or perhaps the way they were raised. Some captivity can be severe, while some is less obvious.

> Sometimes it takes a lifetime for all your defenses to break down before you realize: this is not how I want to live!

Some people are captive to a lifestyle that is haphazard and disorganized. They just can't quite get ahead in life because they can't ever seem to do simple things like find their car keys in the morning. Did you know that some captivity appears humorous like that? For example, years of driving an old smelly car held together by duct tape can start to tamper with your confidence. Eventually, you start to think you aren't worth anything better.

Whatever the enemy is using to steal your joy and defeat you, know this: God wants to give you the ability to stop that interference now and in the future! You see, when you are being tampered with, you may not even realize it until you find yourself in the middle of a mess. Of course, you may have lived with the mess for so long that you have just learned to be comfortable with how things are.

When something is *tampered* with, it's different than something boldly breaking in to change things. Tampering sneaks in a little bit at a time, quietly picking the lock, sneaking in the back door, until you wake up one day and wonder where your sense of security went.

Sometimes it takes a lifetime for all your defenses to break down before you realize: this is not how I want to live!

Humanity Captive

Genesis 3:15 was probably the single most pivotal and intriguing prophecy of human history. One simple, mysterious statement uttered from the mouth of God was to be the ultimate declaration of war to break the inward struggle that exists in every human heart—the struggle of man fighting his way out of desperate, spiraling-out-of-control circumstances. The verse says:

> And I will put enmity between thee and the woman, and between thy seed and her seed; it shall bruise thy head, and thou shalt bruise his heel.

God boldly gave this prophecy to the serpent that had worked his way into the garden and stripped Adam and Eve of their dreams. Surely, at that moment, Adam and Eve must have stood wondering, "How could this have happened?" It was not supposed to work out that way. They had such a promised future to experience. Until that fateful day, they had joy, riches, provision, and great expectations before them.

"It's not fair," they must have thought. "If only we had seen this coming!" The trickery had worked perfectly, and now they were slaves to a set of unexpected circumstances. Where once stood a beautiful future filled with big dreams, now stood only broken dreams, dust, and ashes. Without question, Adam and Eve desperately wished they could rewind time just a few hours and start over. Perhaps this tragedy could have been prevented. Now what was going to happen? Something was different, for sure, and they were caged in surroundings they could not change.

These two original human beings were not going to be the only ones who watched their big dreams crumble all around them. Millions of men, women, and children have followed them into the pages of history, wishing that their lives were in a different set of circumstances too. Some situations are the direct result of our own choices, while others were handed to us because of the choice of someone else. In either case, for many, the lifestyle of captivity has continued for so long that most don't know anything different. The children of Adam and Eve, for instance, were never going to know or relate to what their parents had once enjoyed. Those children were born in captivity.

Certainly the devil reveled in the sense of accomplishment that came from Adam and Eve's failure. It was his reigning moment of retaliation and an opportunity to set a cycle in motion. Instead of Adam and Eve living the life of liberty and joy that God intended for them, the serpent tampered with their destiny and handed them a counterfeit way of life.

Of course, Satan's evil intentions extended far beyond Adam and Eve. It was at least three generations after Noah and the Flood when a boy would be born who decided he wanted to build an empire. His name was Nimrod. (See Genesis 10–11.)

> Some situations are the direct result of our own choices, while others were handed to us because of the choice of someone else.

Like the serpent in the garden, Nimrod too loved the sense of accomplishment that came from handing out promises of fortune. A skilled hunter, he deeply enjoyed the applause of people who praised his great feats of hunting the wild beasts of the land. As Nimrod grew, he wanted more of men's adoration and would find cunning ways to keep the people around him impressed. He wanted to do big things and be praised for them. His thirst for glory would ultimately make him hunt for the devotion of men's hearts, and he would use riches and promises of pleasure to keep them coming for more. His tactics made him the world's first great emperor.

Nimrod built many cities. His greatest accomplishment was the luxurious city of Babel—later called Babylon. The people had such a sense of pride about the city that they built the well-known Tower of Babel. It was extremely impressive, and people began to see this new King Nimrod as a god. Instead of remembering the true God and creator of the universe, people lusted for the fruit and delicacies Nimrod's Babylon had to offer.

Little did they know, however, that Babylon would eventually bring them sorrow as their new king began to demand total loyalty and dependence through tactics of control and fear. It's no wonder that the names Babel and Babylon mean "confusion." It is confusing when you are expecting blessing but keep getting hit with repeated disappointment. This is what the world, or Babylon, does to people's lives. It deceives them. Babylon is described this way in Revelation 18:14: "And the fruits that thy soul lusted after are departed from thee, and all things which were dainty and goodly are departed from thee, and thou shalt find them no more at all."

Nimrod became the figure that would be the root of all idolatry and occultism. He was the embodiment of the serpent in the garden who coveted the devotion of men's hearts and promised them protection and prosperity in exchange for it, although attached to his gifts and pleasures in Babylon were also abuses, emptiness, and disappointments—things this deceiver failed to mention to Adam and Eve when he used the same false promises in the Garden of Eden. Typical for victims of abuse, people there began to believe in total dependence on their abuser. The color and lights of comfort and fleshly pleasure would dazzle one human life after another. Even though it left them empty and confused, they kept being tempted with more and more, believing they would eventually find their day of fortune.

So they worshiped Nimrod until time and practice taught the world that this was the acceptable way of life. Nimrod imparted what we know today as a worldly mind-set. People became servants to this worldly system called Babylon.

While the physical city of Babylon has come and gone, the Babylonian system is still the way of the world.

This Babylonian system has many methods of tampering with us and keeping us from living as God intends. Yet even living with its disappointments and frustrations, many won't look for a way out because it is the only sense of security and culture they know. And as Nimrod carefully calculated, this practice of captivity to the system would be repeated again and again. Deliverance would take someone stepping in to paint a different picture, someone who would help people see that they could have something far more rewarding. Someone had to let them know that their lives were being tampered with.

So God began to change things with one word—one simple prophecy that would make a way to stop the cycle. He let Lucifer and all created beings know that Jesus was coming and He would crush the head of Nimrod's Babylon. Then we would have the power to stand up and interrupt our own cycle of human captivity.

Up From the Dust

Today many people only know the captivity of Babylon. What I mean by this is that they have become so used to the things that are not right, they don't even realize when something is wrong. Their lives are filled with broken dreams, dust, and ashes, but they feel powerless to do anything about it. Their once promised future lies in rubble all around them. They wish they didn't have a broken heart or feelings of bitterness. They wish they lived in a better house or had a better job. They wish they could quit sinning. They wish they could fix their marriage. And the list goes on and on. Yet if we stay in that state long enough, we accept our Babylon as normal and pass on that mind-set to future generations.

Living in Babylon does not mean you came from a history of total addiction or demon possession. It means you have grown to accept and depend on habits, goals, lifestyles, and mind-sets that God never intended. Therefore you continually have to relearn dependence on the ways of God over the ways of the world. Each of us has come out of a different lifestyle, background, and set of circumstances—much of which was patterned by the world's culture. Your background and circumstances are different from anyone else's. These varying circumstances can form patterns inside us that we begin to view as normal or accept as though they are God's position on things.

Yet at some point we have to say, "This is not God's best for me. Somewhere an enemy crept in." The key is knowing that when your life has been tampered with by the devil, God always has a tailor-made way to bring you *out of the dust*. You may be down right now, but God is in the business of picking you up. He wants to show you how to destroy every ounce of captivity that has tampered with your destiny—your blessing.

Think about Adam and Eve in the garden. Even when they made the worst decision of their lives and ate the forbidden fruit, God had an immediate solution to their dilemma. Their lives had suffered a horrible interference. But God stepped in and provided the road to deliverance. That is proof enough that it doesn't matter how your captivity came.

Perhaps your circumstance was handed to you unfairly, or maybe you eagerly jumped into it with both feet. You must come to know, however, that God is standing in *your garden* with a promise of deliverance for you today—the same way He did for Adam and Eve. God promised them a Deliverer who would pay back the enemy that forced his way into their lives.

Genesis 3:15 is the prophecy showing us the way that God

made for us to reclaim what Babylon unjustly took away. Jesus is the fulfillment of that prophecy. He is the way out of our Babylonian captivity, and He wants to teach every Christian the art of rising up in His power to come out of the dust. We just have to learn to walk it out and recapture our possessions, our confidence, our dignity, and our peace.

If we will allow Him to, the Lord will anoint us to experience a life of total power—the way He originally intended. I believe it can be so supernatural that it will be as if your past of captivity never happened. You can live as though that person never hurt you—looking on the memories as if it happened to someone else. This is entirely possible because the Bible calls Jesus the second Adam: "And so it is written, The first man Adam was made a living soul; the last Adam was made a quickening spirit" (1 Cor. 15:45). In other words, this verse is saying that, yes, Adam was alive. But Jesus was not only living—He also gave life!

Jesus came to give Adam a "do-over." Even though the devil thought he enjoyed victory in the Garden of Eden, God still got what He originally intended. Satan didn't take into account that there was going to be another Adam, and this one wouldn't fail the test. That was just how the Lord crushed Satan's head. Jesus interrupted the cycle of captivity that was once set in motion, and He is handing us the power to break the cycle in our own lives. Jesus is providing life—power to give you a new sense of purpose no matter what you did wrong or what bad thing has happened to you. You can step

> If we will allow Him to, the Lord will anoint us to experience a life of total power. It will be as if your past of captivity never happened.

into God's supernatural power and enjoy the new way of thinking that will resurrect you *from the dust*!

A Fridge Full of Rotten Leftovers

Now I don't know about you, but my least favorite day is grocery day. That is because grocery day means work—a lot of work—and it takes the whole family. The worst part of it is the refrigerator full of leftovers that have to be removed before the new groceries can be placed in it. You know, all those containers that made their way to the back of the fridge so long ago that you don't even remember putting them in there. Now it's time to open each one and clean it out. Oh, you just don't want to face up to it. Then there's the produce drawer. Yeah, I think that used to be lettuce, but now it looks more like a bag of some strange brown liquid. *Ugh!* Yet the only way to get rid of it is to address each item, one by one, smell by smell. I dread the fridge full of leftovers, but I know that unless I address the fridge, I will not have room for the new food I am planning to buy.

> When Jesus rose from the dead, He gave us His power to remove each chain of Babylonian captivity and fill us with great glory in its place.

God begins the supernatural process of bringing you up from the dust and ashes by removing the leftovers that Babylon has left behind. The Lord doesn't make you eat and relive the leftovers. No! He wants to remove them. Yet it isn't good enough for Him to just remove them for you. He wants you to remove them with His power and help—supernaturally. That is the way of the Holy Spirit. He works within us and through us. This principle is found all through the Bible—men and women working with God, and God working with them.

If the Lord wants to work through you to remove the leftovers of your life, it means you will have to face what lives in you. Just like the old food in the fridge that you don't want to see or smell, the leftovers of Babylon in our lives will have to be addressed. *Ugh*...again!

Who wants to do it? God does. But He *won't* do it *without* you. That means we will have to admit to some things and face them. Have you ever noticed how other people close to us can notice our little personality quirks and bad habits? Often it seems everyone sees them but us. Then when someone is finally bold enough to mention them, we respond by saying, "I don't do that," or "I am not like that." Then we think no one understands our point of view or we are just being misunderstood.

This scenario is the chasm that stands in the middle of many marriages. We think our spouse doesn't understand where we are coming from when often they are just responding to that little bit of Babylon that is coming out of us. It's the habit toward certain kinds of captivity that we grew up with. It is usually passed down from parents who learned it from their parents and beyond.

These are the leftovers that God wants to remove from us so we can be filled with the fruit of the Spirit, the power of God, and His glory. It may certainly be a nasty mess to remove, but that mess will only last a short time. Then the fridge gets wiped out with disinfectant and prepared for a bounty of new and fresh substance. When Jesus rose from the dead, He gave us His power to remove each chain of Babylonian captivity and fill us with great glory in its place. Of course, it would be wonderful if doing that was as easy as an afternoon of cleaning the refrigerator. But the best part is that, if you are willing, God will give you supernatural power to do it for the long haul. Let God open your eyes and begin bringing you up from the dust. Become willing to address some Babylonian leftovers in your life. God will take His time, breaking each link in the chain of your captivity one by one—very carefully so that you are aware of them. Then He will strengthen you to be permanently free from Babylon.

Ask for Directions to Zion

God doesn't care for the spirit of Babylon, and His mission is to defeat its presence in our lives. The prophet Jeremiah gives us a clear picture of how God defeated the city of Babylon: "Declare ye among the nations, and publish, and set up a standard; publish, and conceal not: say, Babylon is taken, Bel is confounded, Merodach is broken in pieces; her idols are confounded, her images are broken in pieces" (Jer. 50:2).

It is obvious that God does not like the presence of Babylon because it represents everything that is defiant and set against Him. It is the epitome of sin. In Jeremiah 50:2, God makes it well known that He wants Babylon to be taken out. He was telling you and me that He wants to take Babylon's spirit of captivity completely out of our lives. And He is still telling you today that every bad habit, demonic bondage, and mental image that this spirit has imbedded into your life is about to be destroyed. Don't try to hide it, but let it be known that God is breaking the spirit of Babylonian captivity off you.

But the Lord can only do it if you allow Him to. You have to want to come out of the dust. Does that mean you just want to be relieved from the effects of the dust? No. You have to pick up and move to a new location.

After Jeremiah prophesied against Babylon in chapter 50, he gave the picture of what God's people were supposed to do in order to get out of that place. Jeremiah 50:4–5 says, "In those days, and in that time, saith the LORD, the children of Israel shall come, they and the children of Judah together, going and weeping: they shall go, and seek the LORD their God. They *shall ask the way to Zion* with their faces thitherward, saying, Come, and let us join ourselves to the LORD in a perpetual covenant that shall not be forgotten" (emphasis added). The prophet told them that since Babylon was being destroyed, it was time to get out. While this was an actual account in the history of Israel, it is a prophetic example of us being delivered from the captivity of the world we have come to know and become so accustomed to.

It is obvious the way to get out of Babylon is to begin by asking directions. That is why the verse says they will "ask the way to Zion." Zion is the picture of deliverance. It is the place of holiness. We need to ask God to give us directions to Zion. If you want to clean out the leftovers and flee the captivity of the past that keeps defeating the present, then ask for directions to Zion. You leave captivity first by seeking God about your issues; then you ask Him to teach you how to find the way to Zion. To me it is just like following the instructions of a global positioning system (GPS) in your car. You locate your current position on the screen and do nothing more than follow each direction as it is given. You don't try to see the final destination first!

For some reason we have trouble approaching God that way. We always want Him to tell us about our future in detail, while He just wants us to locate where we are now and then let Him give us each direction one step at a time. For example, we want to find the instant way out of debt when God wants to teach us how to tithe or give an offering. Coming out of the dust is a process, and it begins by asking the Lord to help you find the way to Zion. That is the first "direction" He is waiting for you to do.

As you leave each area of past captivity, there may be some weeping along the way: "...going and weeping: they shall go, and seek the Lord their God" (Jer. 50:4). But the road to Zion puts you in a place of strength with God. Verse 5 says it gives you a perpetual covenant or an ongoing relationship with God that won't leave you easily when new worldly trials and temptations try to enter your life. It isn't always so easy to leave the only way of living you have ever known, even as a Christian who loves the Lord. If you are used to responding to life through bitterness, then it can be difficult to walk a new road to Zion that has a joyful perspective.

You can ask God for your own directions to Zion. He will show you each step to bring you out of Babylon. Jeremiah 50:8 says, "Remove out of the midst of Babylon, and go forth out of the land of the Chaldeans, and be as the he goats before the flocks." We have to choose to leave our past habits of captivity and run toward Zion. The male goats in this verse represent those who lead the way. They take the initiative to get the job done and set an example for others to follow even through rocky ground. Take the initiative to flee from the chains of your Babylon. Get behind the wheel and follow God's spiritual GPS. He will give it to you if you are willing to ask Him, and you will find your way out of your past of dust and ashes. You don't have to figure out all the details right now; just follow each step as God shows you the way into Zion!

My Babylon Is Too Big

Many years ago, I remember walking through a time when we had so many trials and disappointments while trying to find our way into the ministry that it seemed like we were in total failure. During that time, my husband described to our pastor how we were feeling. "I feel like we are in a tornado of circumstances," he explained. "Everything is coming at me so fast, and I can't slow down from all the storms. Then every once in a while one of my arms will stick out of the cyclone, and I will feel a brief moment of relief until it gets sucked back in again. Then another limb will stick out for a little rest, and then it gets pulled in again as the storm continues."

> You don't have to figure out all the details right now; just follow each step as God shows you the way.

I am sure you have been there too! We had financial troubles, failed attempts toward ministry, and a whole host of frustrated emotions.

We were fighting so many battles we didn't know where to start. Our attitude was, "Forget trying to work on the fruit of the Spirit and removing past leftovers; we are too busy just trying to fix the present mess, eat, and pay the rent." We felt captive to failure.

Sometimes it looks like the Babylon you have to flee from is just too big to overcome. For some people it is a mountain of debt. For others it is the pain of past abuse preventing them from correctly responding to life. Maybe it is the lifestyle of poverty, addiction, and instability. Maybe it is one failed business attempt after another, or a lack of skill and education holding you back. It could be the frustration of a sin habit, anger, fear, or bitterness. Many hold the disappointment of betrayal or divorce. Some are captive to social status, race, and nationality. While many Christians try hard to love and serve the Lord, they just don't know how to live outside of Babylon. They can't see the other side because their Babylon is looming like a large dark cloud over them every day. To add to that, demons love to hang around in an effort to keep you feeling hopeless even though you know and love the Lord.

God wants every believer to progress in their Christianity far beyond the peace of knowing we are forgiven of our sin and that someday heaven will be our home. He also wants us to grow beyond going to church and hearing a great sermon that does little to transform us for more than a week or two. God wants you to see that your habits of captivity can be overcome.

Powerfully enough, God planted the greatest example of overcoming the impossibilities of life in the Book of Nehemiah. Here the people of God were living captive to Babylon—just as many of God's people do today because they have yet to learn a new way of living. They know that God has something better for them but struggle to get there. They say, "Amen!" to the messages of healing and deliverance at church. They shout and sing. Yet they go home and are hit in the face with the reality of circumstances.

Some people look around to see the same lack of money in the checking account. Others see the same unsaved spouse bound to drugs. There sits a wayward teenager whose rebellion is wreaking havoc on the family. The cigarettes so hated are still on one person's counter, while the reality of their failing business is threatening to take the house away. For many good Christian people, a "Babylon too big" is far too real. But this is nothing new to God. He walked a man named Nehemiah through the very same situation. This is the story that holds the answers to rising out of captivity when the dreams of your life are falling apart.

A Stolen Heritage and Promises Tampered With

The words of Nehemiah...Hanani, one of my brethren, came, he and certain men of Judah; and I asked them concerning the Jews that had escaped, which were left of the captivity, and concerning Jerusalem. And they said unto me, The remnant that are left of the captivity there in the province are in great affliction and reproach: the wall of Jerusalem also is broken down, and the gates thereof are burned with fire.

—NEHEMIAH 1:1–3

Nehemiah couldn't believe what he was hearing. The heritage he knew was gone. All he loved was stolen and taken away. Could the report be true? Maybe he heard it wrong. Perhaps it was the wrong information. He had only asked about his friends and family back home. Nehemiah wanted to hear about all his brothers who had remained in Jerusalem when most of Israel was taken captive into Babylon. Yet he couldn't believe his ears when he heard the stories of pain, affliction, broken buildings, and fires. Nothing was left of God's remnant back home, even though they had managed to escape being taken. They were still afflicted by the Babylonian attack, and all the prosperity they knew was now lost.

The report Nehemiah received detailed three tragic events and painted a perfect picture of the moments of letdown and broken dreams every person has experienced at some point. These are the experiences that make it easy to feel like life is unfair and, of course, to accept the old questions asking, "God, where were You when that happened to me?"

The first thing the report told Nehemiah was the condition of the people. They were afflicted or experiencing a tremendous amount of trouble. That is what it means to be afflicted. It means to walk through problem after problem with little time for relief. The people were also in reproach, which means they were disgraced. This speaks of not only a lot of problems, but also to feel totally humiliated during it. Imagine such great trouble that leaves you feeling horribly embarrassed in front of neighbors and friends.

> Remember, Satan is the thief. He tampers with what does not belong to him. He will try to burn down gates and break in illegally! That is what thieves do.

Secondly, this Scripture passage speaks of the wall of Jerusalem being broken down, meaning that their defenses were compromised. Doesn't that sound like many Christians? They walk through many disgraceful problems and then don't have the wherewithal to defend themselves against the onslaught.

Then thirdly, Nehemiah heard that the gates of the city were burned with fire. This is clearly an example of demonic forces trespassing on our lives. Gates speak of an entry point. They reveal the places where the devil finds access.

That does not necessarily mean that we gave him that access!

Here Scripture says the gates were burned down forcefully, not opened for entry. And in John 10:10 the Bible says, "The thief cometh not, but for to steal, and to kill, and to destroy." Remember, Satan is the thief. He tampers with what does not belong to him, and he doesn't always find a *legal* entry. He will try to burn down gates and break in illegally! That is what thieves do. Remember, Adam and Eve didn't really give Satan access to the garden. They just didn't kick him out when they met up with him. It was their garden, and the devil snuck into it uninvited!

In a nutshell, Nehemiah found his heritage full of problems, he was completely humiliated, and there was no solution for victory. The worst was, all of it was now tampered with by enemy forces and was under their control. Now if that doesn't speak to some point in all our lives, nothing can. Everyone has been messed with like that. Maybe your whole life has felt that way, or maybe just one or two areas. Regardless, we can learn from Nehemiah's powerful response.

From Weeping to Warfare in One Prayer

Of course, Nehemiah's reaction to this news began the same way many of us respond to tragedies, disappointments, or other hard circumstances. Nehemiah 1:4 says, "And it came to pass, when I heard these words, that I sat down and wept, and mourned certain days...." So his initial response was a normal one. First, he sat down. We usually sit down when we feel hopeless and tired of trying. Sitting down is an action of retreat. Then the crying began. When things are going badly, we cry. Well, maybe women cry, but men cry too—sometimes differently, but they cry. Some crying comes out in anger with tirades of complaints, but it's still crying.

Nehemiah cried when his lifelong dreams were tampered with,

and he did it for "certain days." Now I don't know how long "certain days" were exactly, but it definitely lasted for more than one day.

Maybe Nehemiah reported his tears lasting a vague number of days (plural) because it was a longer amount of time than he wanted to admit. Have you ever been there? I would say that he was pretty down in the dumps, for sure.

> We cannot change the past, but we can change our future. Changing your future begins in prayer.

Then, suddenly he did something in the middle of his tears. He "...fasted, and prayed before the God of heaven" (Neh. 1:4). He could have blamed God, as many people do. He could have played the victim and asked why again and again. Instead of assuming that God deserted his dreams, he decided God was the answer to fulfilling them. Not only was it amazing that Nehemiah prayed while he was discouraged, but the real power existed in *what* he prayed. His detailed prayer transformed him from weeping into warfare. It was the defining moment that started the process of rebuilding the dreams Babylon had destroyed.

Yes, Nehemiah could have kept on crying. He could have easily stayed depressed. It is easy to stay depressed when you feel hopeless because emotions can come on you like roaring water and almost paralyze you. Bad news can make you suddenly feel like you have been punched in the stomach. Yet this simple man found a prayer inside himself that changed everything. Now he had to choose to move beyond these tragic events so that he could address a solution for the future. As the old saying goes, we cannot change the past, but we can change our future. Changing your future begins in prayer, but not any kind of prayer. It begins with pivotal and accurate prayers.

God wants us to pray from our heart about any situation we face. According to the Bible, however, there are only certain prayers that cause Him to listen and respond. First John 5:14–15 says, "And this is the confidence that we have in him, that, if we ask any thing *according to his will*, he heareth us: And if we know that he hear us, whatsoever we ask, we know that we have the petitions that we desired of him" (emphasis added). If you feel unsure whether God is listening to your prayers, go back to reflect on the direct truths of these scriptures. They tell us that there is a way to feel confident about your prayers. I want to feel confident when I pray, don't you? Many times when people are in trouble, they pray "hit-and-miss" prayers, just hoping something good will happen. God wants you to be confident about your prayers so that when you walk away from your prayer closet, you have a deep knowing that something happened in the realm of the spirit that will turn your life around.

The first way to have confidence when you come to God is by praying in line with His will. If you aren't sure what that is, then just make sure you pray in a way that agrees with the Bible. Study how people of the Bible got answers to prayers. We cannot just pray according to our personal preference based on how we feel at the moment. God has a pattern for successful prayer that will work in both good times and bad. Be biblical and purposeful about your prayers, and then you will develop the confidence that God is listening. Once that happens, the Bible is clear that we will get exactly what we are praying. Now I say, "Amen!" to that.

Nehemiah 1:5–11 quotes the confident prayer of Nehemiah. I want to explore the details of his prayer here because it is a prayer that can resurrect broken dreams. You can use it as a pattern for your situation. There are five key points to his prayer I want you to see, and if you will put them into practice, your prayers will turn you around too.

He didn't blame God.

"…O Lord God of heaven…that keepeth covenant and mercy for them that love him and observe his commandments" (v. 5). Rather than question God or blame Him for why he was in this horrible mess, Nehemiah reminded himself that God never breaks a promise. This is probably the first and foremost important key to coming out of a Babylon of broken dreams—when you can still see the God who keeps His promises. A vast majority of people cannot do that when they are disappointed. Nehemiah immediately reaffirmed that God is faithful to His Word. It is easy to question the promises of God when things don't work out the way you expect. Rise up in prayer, and remind yourself that God always keeps His promises and that what has happened in your life is not because He failed to come through for you. God does not fail those who love and serve Him.

He expected the Lord to listen to His prayer.

"Let thine ear now be attentive, and thine eyes open, that thou mayest hear the prayer of thy servant, which I pray before thee now..." (v. 6). Nehemiah was bold enough to ask the Lord to listen to his prayer. In fact, he expected it. He didn't assume the natural route that God had overlooked him. He expected God to pay attention to what he had to say. Nehemiah requested that the Lord open His divine eyes and ears so He could hear his prayer. Now that's confidence!

He repented for his sins and the sins of the people.

"...I pray before thee now, day and night, for the children of Israel thy servants, and confess the sins of the children of Israel, which we have sinned against thee: both I and my father's house have sinned" (v. 6). Every prayer during a serious trial involves some form of repentance. Pride always wants us to assume we did everything right and that it was God's fault, or that God was the one who didn't do anything when our life was tampered with. Nehemiah was not afraid to admit he had faults that contributed to the present tragedy. He didn't act like the pitiful victim, but he simply acknowledged his failure. Not only was he not afraid to admit failure, but he also detailed it. He stated that he lived corruptly and didn't keep God's Word. I don't believe acknowledging the specifics of your mistakes and sins is important because God wants us to revel in them or feel hopelessly beat up over them. Instead, God wants to cultivate in us an awareness of them so we avoid making the same errors in the future. This man was not afraid to admit that there were areas in his life where he didn't keep the commandments of God as he should.

He believed in the forgiveness of God.

"But if ye turn unto me, and keep my commandments, and do them; though there were of you cast out unto the uttermost part of the heaven, yet will I gather them from thence, and will bring them unto the place that I have chosen to set my name there" (v. 9). He purposely reminded himself, as well as the Lord, of God's promises to extend great mercy when we turn back to Him. No matter what seems to have fallen apart, God has committed Himself to repair each broken piece if we ask Him for forgiveness. The Lord will take all the scattered events that don't make sense and pull them back together. When He does, you will become a place where His name and presence can live. You have to believe in the forgiveness of God and that He will pull your lifelong dreams together. All it requires is that you turn toward the Lord, not away from Him, especially when you feel like you have blown it.

He expected God to manifest supernatural power.

"Now these are thy servants and thy people, whom thou hast redeemed by thy great power, and by thy strong hand" (v. 10). You have to believe God will manifest His anointing for you. Nehemiah expected God's strong hand to come through, even though the people had failed. It is sometimes easy to believe the Lord will manifest miracles for someone else, but we see ourselves less deserving. Often we just hope that "maybe" God will cause a breakthrough. No, you have to see that the strong hand of the Lord is there to operate *just for you.* One of the main reasons we don't come out of the dust and ashes of Babylon is because we don't believe God will manifest miracles. If we actually believed it, we would talk and act like it. Many people talk more about their disappointments and the impossibilities. We say words like "I feel so frustrated," or "I am overwhelmed," and "I can't take it anymore." Those words reflect that we have given up. You have to believe God's power will work for you if you want to be free from the captivity in your life.

How Did This Happen?

Whether you have been a Christian for years or maybe didn't know the Lord until later in life, it is likely there have been times you have asked God why some things turned out the way they did. Perhaps it was a healing that didn't happen or a relationship that fell apart. Maybe it was a financial issue. I am sure Adam and Eve asked that question many times over. I am even more certain that they cried uncontrollably over it.

Yet coming out of Babylon means you cannot keep looking back toward it. Simply recognize the negative habits Babylon created in you, and then start moving toward Zion so you can be free from them. If you spend a great deal of time overreflecting on the past, you will never live free in the future.

> It is sometimes easy to believe the Lord will manifest miracles for someone else. You have to see that the strong hand of the Lord is there to operate *just for you.*

During my years in ministry, I have known so many people who have looked at their disappointments and felt like they did everything they knew to prevent them, but they still experienced some form of letdown. They just kept asking, "Why did this happen?"

Well, there are millions of ways we could answer that question, and I don't want to exhaust every viewpoint. I do, however, want to give you one simple solution here. Whatever you do, never assume you did everything correctly all the time. This is such a major area where we miss it because we want to shift blame—usually to God. Now, that does not mean you go the other way and beat *yourself* up thinking you are a total failure. What it means is stop holding on to the idea that you did everything you knew, and now you can't understand why God allowed this to happen.

Remember, no matter what, it is *never* God's fault! Even if you were unjustly used and abused by someone else, God cannot be blamed. The Lord is not your problem. He is always your answer!

Adam and Eve could have blamed God for "letting" the serpent enter the garden and topple their world. That mind-set will not get you anywhere near freedom. Once you can eliminate any question about that, you are well on your way to being free from the captivity of the past. When your life was tampered with, it happened. Now it's over. Yes, it may hurt. But you now have to focus on the solution that will keep Satan out of your life from this point forward. This is where true healing begins.

Realize that in this world there are trials that come straight from the devil, just as they did for Adam and Eve. We will never live without tests and trials here on this earth. What we can learn, however, is how to defeat the lifestyle and captivity of Babylon and live in victory. Remember, this is a process of learning. Growth in this area does not happen overnight or because you heard one sermon about taking authority over the devil. Jesus taught this so powerfully when He said, "I have told you these things, so that in Me you may have [perfect] peace and confidence. In the world you have tribulation and trials and distress and frustration; but be of good cheer [take courage; be confident, certain, undaunted]! For I have overcome the world. [I have deprived it of power to harm you and have conquered it for you.]" (John 16:33, AMP).

The word *overcome* in that verse means "to prevail over an enemy."

Jesus found the answer to defeat every trial and frustration. He has deprived the world (Babylon) of its ability to harm you. Realize that He lives inside you and will teach you everything He knows. Therefore keep doing what you have learned, and when something doesn't work out the way you expect, ask the Lord to teach you how to grow. With time, you will learn to gain victories over areas you previously struggled with.

It's Time to Kick the Habit

The Book of Nehemiah takes place during a time in Israel's history when they were taken as captives to Babylon. It happened because they had sinned against the Lord again and again. Finally the Lord allowed them to be taken into captivity. This captivity of Israel is a blueprint for coming out of any kind of bondage or pain regardless of how you got there. Again, sometimes it is the result of our own choices and sometimes the choice of someone else.

Israel was in captivity for seventy years. That means there were people born while they were in that captivity, and those people never knew anything else. They were accustomed to a Babylonian way of life. Even though we are Christians, we live in the natural world and are very accustomed to a worldly (Babylonian) way of life. Therefore God wants to teach us how to come out of worldly captivity and worldly mind-sets—He wants to show us another way to live. For example, if you only know what it is like to live in a broken-down shack without running water, then you are going to have some trouble if someone hands you the

> We will never live without tests and trials here on this earth. What we can learn, however, is how to defeat the lifestyle and captivity of Babylon and live in victory.

keys to a mansion. It would take a great deal of retraining for you to learn palace living.

This is why simple deliverance prayers to remove strongholds are not enough. Yes, we *need* deliverance prayers to remove the influence of evil spirits. Once the spirits are gone, however, you have to know how to live a whole new lifestyle without them. A lot of people have learned to depend on their captivity by force of habit. Then when the demons are gone, they lose their source or sense of security and what was familiar to them. That is why so many people go back into bondage.

Matthew 12:43–45 says, "When the unclean spirit is gone out of a man, he walketh through dry places, seeking rest, and findeth none. Then he saith, I will return into my house from whence I came out; and when he is come, he findeth it empty, swept, and garnished. Then goeth he, and taketh with himself seven other spirits more wicked than himself, and they enter in and dwell there: and the last state of that man is worse than the first. Even so shall it be also unto this wicked generation." What was Jesus really trying to say here? Notice He said the evil spirit returns to "his house." Now, when you have lived in a house for a long time, that home starts to look like you, it smells like your things (good or bad), and it reflects your tastes and styles because it is your house. Even if you move out, it still looks like you. When new owners move in, it takes time for them to "make it their own."

It is this way when demons are forced out of our lives too. We have to remodel the house that looks, smells, and reflects the demonic darkness of Babylon. In fact, when you move to Zion, you can't build a Babylonian-style house! When we change the look of our dwelling, demons will try to return. But they won't recognize the place. They quickly realize that it is not a place they can inhabit. The stuff they like is no longer there. It doesn't reflect them anymore.

This is what I mean by saying we need to learn palace living, or better said, we need to learn Zion living over the life culture of Babylon.

Demons won't keep coming back when you move out of Babylon and head for Zion. If your life has been tampered with, leaving you with some broken dreams, dust, and ashes, then know today that Jesus is giving you new directions to come out. Get ready to leave the captive lifestyle, no matter how big or small you are when coming out. Your days of living with the ashes and leftovers are over!

Shake thyself from the dust; arise; and sit down, O Jerusalem: loose thyself from the bands of thy neck, O captive daughter of Zion.

[ISAIAH 52:2]

CHAPTER 2

DECIDE YOUR SEASON of CHANGE

URING MY YEARS OF MINISTERING TO PEOPLE, ONE
common thing I have noticed is how many Christians have
the tendency to *wish* for, rather than *create*, their breakthrough. They desperately want God to do something with their life
or a specific situation they are facing, when really God wants *them* to
do something. When the odds seem stacked against them, they sit
back and hope or wish for a miracle.

The reason some prison inmates break out of prison is because
they are constantly looking for an opportunity despite the odds against
them. They are so determined to make that break that they spend every
waking hour making connections, gathering information, and then
creating and collecting the necessary tools. They look for opportunities to escape their present captivity. Sometimes they plan for months
or longer, and they work hard at it. Then they determine the time and
the place of the break. They decide on their day of "breakthrough"
because they are not content to live under the present conditions.

God has breathed into the human spirit the determination to
pursue life and freedom. People have been known to go beyond natural
means and stretch the limit of human capability to find it. Therefore

if natural prisoners can create a break from natural captivity, or if armed forces troops can find a way out of difficult situations, what can we accomplish for our spiritual freedom using the anointing? Imagine the demonic strongholds we could pull down and the miracles we could produce if we would just take hold of the opportunity.

> God has breathed into the human spirit the determination to pursue life and freedom. People have been known to go beyond natural means and stretch the limit of human capability to find it.

During World War II, the Nazi high command decided it was wasting too many of its resources on prisoner of war (POW) escapees, and they began to clamp down on the security measures of its prison camps. So they took some of the prisoners with the greatest records of escape to the infamous Stalag Luft III prison. British squadron leader Roger Bushell was among them. The leader of a secret prison escape committee, Bushell was known as "Big X" and had a history of attempted prison escape operations. Upon coming to the Stalag Luft III compound, Bushell was under extreme threat by the Germans that should he escape again, he would immediately be executed.

Stalag Luft III was one of the largest German prison camps, housing nearly ten thousand Allied prisoners toward the end of the war. Carefully designed to discourage escapes, it was located in a remote area approximately one hundred miles southeast of Berlin and considered ideal because it was seen as a difficult area from which to flee. Now consider the incredible odds stacked against any prisoner even considering breaking out. One of the most common ways prisoners escaped from POW camps was through tunneling.

Prisoners would dig secret tunnels underground to make their way from the camp.

This camp made tunneling difficult, if not impossible. The prisoners' barracks were constructed aboveground so that guards would more easily detect any tunneling activities. The camp was also located in an area with sandy subsoil that was yellowish in color and easily seen if dug up because the surface soil was more of a gray color. Either was easily recognizable if seen on a prisoner's clothing or piled on the grounds. In addition, sand is extremely difficult to work with in creating any type of stable tunnel. The Nazis also placed seismographic microphones around the camp so they would be able to detect the sounds of any tunneling activity.

Then in 1943, "Big X" conceived a plot to break out approximately two hundred fifty prisoners from the camp. His secret committee planned three tunnels famously known as Tom, Dick, and Harry. Tunnel entrances were carefully selected to keep them hidden from the guards. To remain undetected by perimeter microphones, the tunnels were dug thirty feet below the surface—an amazing depth if you think about it!

The tunnels were very small, measuring only about two feet in diameter. To make the tunnels stable, prisoners gradually salvaged pieces of wood from around the camp, mostly from the mattress supports on their beds. Guards never noted that nearly twelve of the twenty slats on each prisoner's bed had been removed. The prisoners even constructed air chambers and staging areas in the tunnels. What is more unbelievable is that they managed to construct a rail car and an air-pumping ventilation system, and they tapped into the camp's electrical grid so the tunnels would have lighting. Distribution of the displaced dirt and sand was done by putting it into old socks that the prisoners would wear in their pants and would then scatter it as they walked about. They commonly placed the discolored sand under garden soil as the prisoners tended the gardens. When disposal became next to impossible because of the volume of dirt and the risk of guards catching them, the prisoners began using one of the tunnels as a dumping ground for more dirt.

Finally after a year, the tunnel called Harry was completed. So the Great Escape was scheduled for March 24, 1944. Little did the prisoners know that their tunnel had come up short of its required destination to bring them to safety. Of the seventy-six men who made their way into the tunnel, seventy-three were caught by the German guards—fifty were executed, twenty-three were returned to prison camps—and only three actually escaped.

The outcome and repercussions resulting from the escape attempt, however, were the real victory in this story. Investigators of the scene were shocked to find how sophisticated and involved this operation had been and that it had occurred under their close watch. They couldn't believe the sheer magnitude of the plot and that it had gone on for more than a year without discovery. Statistics state that 4,000 bed boards were missing, in addition to 90 double-tier bunks. The prisoners used 52 tables, 34 chairs, 1,699 blankets, and 246 water cans, along with other supplies that the guards never noticed missing in all that time. After the war, nearly all the Gestapo members who had executed the recaptured escapees were themselves eventually tried for war crimes during the well-known Nuremberg trials and later executed by the British government.*

I am sharing the short summary of this amazing story, well known as the Great Escape, to show what God has placed in every human being—the determination to conquer, even when something looks unconquerable. Of course, there were many notable POW escapes during World War II, but taking a close look at this one will help you see what can be done if we are determined to rise from our

---

* F. Fedorowicz, "Stalag Luft 3: The Great Escape," translated by A. Strukowska, research provided by Rob Davis, http://www.b24.net/pow/greatescape.htm (accessed February 19, 2008).

impossibilities. You and I have not been born to accept the negative circumstances of life as they are given to us. We have been created by the living God to take every area of spiritual bondage and weakness and decide our day of breakthrough and season for change.

You Must Decide

If you want to rise out of the dust and ashes from severe disappointment of the past, or even a present problem, then *you must decide* your season of change. You cannot just wait and hope that you will "feel" better one day.

I have found very few stories where that was the case. We had one young lady in our church who was in a deep depression. The only thing she had planned for her future was suicide. She harmed herself and prayed she would die. She assumed God was mad at her, so she thought there was no point in living. She later testified to me that she didn't know for sure how God turned her around. She acknowledged that being in a good church with people who loved and helped her was a primary factor. But she said God had changed her, and, over time, she realized that she didn't want to die anymore. She just felt better one day.

> You and I have not been born to accept the negative circumstances of life. We have been created to take every area of spiritual bondage and weakness and decide our day of breakthrough and season for change.

Yes, it is possible for God to change you so that you just feel better one day. Actually, He does it for all of us as He helps us see life through His eyes. Still, this young girl had to make some decisions. She had to stay with the people who love her—her family and a good church—when she could have run from them all. So even though God changed her, she played a role in her own healing. She stepped into her season of change. The road to change requires that you walk toward change.

You will have to be the one who decides when you want to change and break out. You will have to determine when you want to stop feeling bitter about your upbringing or disillusioned about a prayer that didn't appear to be answered. You will have to decide when you have had enough of broken dreams.

Isaiah 52:1–2 is a powerful and prophetic scripture that details how you can decide your season of change. It says, "Awake, awake; put on thy strength, O Zion; put on thy beautiful garments, O Jerusalem, the holy city: for henceforth there shall no more come into thee the uncircumcised and the unclean. Shake thyself from the dust; arise, and sit down, O Jerusalem: loose thyself from the bands of thy neck, O captive daughter of Zion." The message in these verses is meant for us—the spiritual Zion, the spiritual Jerusalem. Notice that it places the main responsibility for a life of deliverance and victory on what *we decide* to do. It specifically tells us that we have to "shake ourselves from the dust." That is the part I don't always like to hear. How about you? When I am disappointed and frustrated about something in my life, I don't particularly feel empowered to "shake myself" out of it.

One of the greatest battlegrounds in this area is in our mind and our emotions, which we will later discuss in detail. The key is that when the devil, people, and circumstances have messed with your life in some way, you must take the initiative to shake yourself free from it. God is there helping you and doing miracles for you, but it will be to no avail if you refuse to embrace today as your season of change.

For example, have you ever worked on a project or worked hard on something you really wanted to do, but in the end you were personally unhappy with your results? Then person after person can come along and tell you what a wonderful job you did and how great it was, but deep down you don't believe it. Even though you appreciate their compliments, you just don't see the good in your finished work. It is the same way with spiritual things. If we refuse to see ourselves stepping out of captivity, then even God cannot help us find a breakthrough. He can give us promises, prophetic words, friends, and even a good pastor, but we still only respond according to an area of failure or dysfunction.

The children of Israel had the same difficulty. No matter how many miracles, signs, and wonders God did for them, they just couldn't see themselves as anything but slaves and, as a result, were enslaved by every circumstance. They never could expect God's provision to be available when they needed it.

If you have a captive mind-set, perhaps in one or many areas, you will not rise up to shake yourself from the dust. You will never see that your season of change is right before you. Instead, you will find yourself complaining and reverting to a negative outlook or previous method of resolve. You will feel trapped by who you have always been in your life. So how do you get to the point where you can shake yourself free and even

> Our careless words are often one of the main roots of sin contributing to our captivity.

know how to come up from the dust? I believe the verses we read from Isaiah 52:1–2 reveal a step-by-step process that will help you know how to rise up and decide that your season of change is upon you.

"Awake, awake."

The first thing we have to do is see the areas we want changed in our life and admit their existence. We can't pretend they aren't there in hope that they will disappear on their own someday. If you have a worry problem, admit it. If you are lazy, then acknowledge it. Whether it's poverty, anger, addiction, depression, debt, discouragement, pride, disease, jealousy, bitterness, or sadness, see it and know what you must address. Know exactly what you are warring against.

"Put on thy strength, O Zion."

Doing this means you prepare for war. Now that you know what the problem is, it requires you to get your war clothes on. This doesn't mean you will always feel like it. I don't always feel like getting up and getting dressed in the morning, but I do it anyway. Sometimes it means taking one step at a time until I get my bearings. You too may have to begin putting on your heavenly armor one piece at a time (Eph. 6:11–18). The key is to keep yourself in a state of war against the things you want changed. Speak to them, bind their power, and declare that you are victorious.

"Put on thy beautiful garments, O Jerusalem, the holy city."

Your beautiful garments represent the decision to live a holy life-style. What things have you been involved with that could have led to some kind of captivity in your life? That doesn't mean you were responsible for all of it, but it does mean you need to be separated from sinful habits—no matter how large or small they may appear. For example, our careless words are often one of the main roots of sin contributing to our captivity. (See James 3:6.) When you have been "messed with," always choose holiness, no matter what.

"There shall no more come into thee the uncircumcised and the unclean."

This means that you must have faith that your days of struggle and invasion by the devil are over! That does not mean Satan will not try to attack you. But it does mean that from here on out you are poised to stand up and resist in the power of the Lord. You may have been cheated and caught off guard in the past, but now you must trust God's promises that He will not allow the unclean, evil works of the devil to invade you without warning. Since God has made that promise, believe it is true for you personally.

"Shake thyself from the dust."

To shake yourself means that you come to your senses. The Bible says the prodigal son had to come to his senses after living in a season of deception (Luke 15:17). There comes a point when you make a pivotal decision that you will not live under your current conditions, regardless of how they came on you. It means seeing your situation as it really is and not based on your feelings. It may mean you have to completely forgive and release someone who has hurt you, or you may have to just determine to walk a different lifestyle. Regardless, you have to be the one who does the "shaking" if you are going to rise from the dust that Babylon has left behind.

> You may have been cheated and caught off guard in the past, but now you must trust God's promises that He will not allow the unclean, evil works of the devil to invade you without warning.

"Arise, and sit down, O Jerusalem."

To step out of your captivity means you will first have to get up from your location. If you are located in debt and poverty, you have to get up from there. You will have to look for ways of living that do not reflect the lifestyle of lack. It may mean you have to find a new place to live. That does not mean you have to place financial pressure on yourself to do so, but it means you must make a step of total transformation, both spiritually and physically. Work for it every day. Now this is the part of "arise, and sit down" I want you to grasp the most. It is the part that makes you "sit down" in a new place. You have to become comfortable with a new lifestyle and way of living. This can be very difficult to do because, in our human nature, we become very secure with the way we have done things for years, even if it is terribly wrong. "Sitting down" takes you from shack living into palace living. This is a learning process, but it begins with the decision to "sit down" in a brand-new place and never go back.

"Loose thyself from the bands of thy neck."

The New Living Translation states this portion of verse 2 very powerfully. It says, "Remove the chains of slavery from your neck." A chain on your neck speaks of anything that burdens you down. If you have been enslaved to some chain from Babylon, you will have to be the one to remove it—not God, but you! When we are bound to something or experiencing a trial, there are always things we have to remove in order to come out of it. It may be a habit or a wrong attitude. It may be material things or a relationship, but there will be things that you have to do without in order to be free. Things that once sustained you and gave you a sense of comfort will have to be given up. Isn't that what Jesus wanted from the rich young ruler? He wanted him to give away the things he depended on so he could learn the new way of faith. Be willing to make long-term changes in order to have liberty in the Spirit. (See 2 Corinthians 3:17.) Real transformation is when you choose your season of change by making changes in your life.

The Baby Who Didn't Live

Back in the summer of 2000, a wonderful couple in our church was pregnant and ready to have their fifth child. They are people who have served the Lord faithfully for many years, who are committed to church, and who work hard for the kingdom of God. Then in the wee hours of a July morning, we received a call that she had given birth to their full-term baby and no heartbeat was found. Attempts were desperately made to resuscitate their little boy, but that was not going to happen. We hurried to the hospital, doing all we knew to do in prayer, but to no avail. The baby did not live.

I can still see the hospital room so clearly as if it were yesterday. As we entered the room, I remember them sitting there, bewildered, holding their lifeless child. All of our hearts felt broken. Their glorious Christian lives were turned upside down and tampered with by this unexpected tragedy.

The days to follow would test all of us beyond measure. It tested our beliefs, our values, and our attitudes. As their pastors, my husband and I questioned our leadership skills. Did we leave people unprepared? Did we not teach good doctrine or even help them through this the best way possible? We even found ourselves questioning whether we really had any anointing or power for miracles. This family, who also are our friends, found their own minds reeling with doubts and questions. Where was God, whom we love so much, and how could He let this happen? The wife tried to hold on to the verses of Scripture that they stood on so many times before for other things. For a brief time it seemed to help, but there was a deep pain inside her. Of course, being true to character, the devil and his demons also hung around to whisper, lie, and taunt all of our ears.

This precious lady who had lost her child became deeply offended with God. She would say, "Lord, I was living right, doing all the right things I thought I was supposed to do. How could You let this happen to our son?"

Chained by grief, she stayed in a dark place for the next two years. She imagined how she could get in her car and kill herself in a car accident. She began to hate her husband and the church, and she wanted to run from it all. People reached out to both her and her husband. They hugged and loved her the best they could. They never gave up on her. That is what you have to love about the people of God. We may all have some flaws, but when you get involved with a good church, those people are right there to push you to victory and love you through your worst trials!

This woman's husband pushed her to go to church and wouldn't allow her to quit. He brought her to every service, even when it seemed like he had a zombie in tow. Her eyes were dark and her face was stone cold. And she would just sit while the rest of the congregation worshiped God.

Thank God for her husband's determination! This man was always singing with the worship team, and week after week I used to wonder what was going on in his mind as he saw her sitting there from where he was on the stage. She was shutting the entire world out around her and didn't seem to care what people thought or did. It went on and on for months, and we felt such despair.

These are the situations where life gets real. Everything you believe and stand for has been invaded, and you have to decide where you are going from here. Emotions can run so strong that you become physically sick with them. What she originally saw through her ordeal was like a wound that was unconquerable. Finally one day her husband told her, "You know, it's time to sing again."

She later told me, "That was the last thing I wanted to do, but slowly I started trying to sing." There were times as pastors that my husband and I both ministered to her and gave her words from the Lord, thinking it wasn't doing a bit of good. I didn't know it at the time, but later she said, "Pastor Brenda, I started doing the things the Lord told me in those prophecies. You told me to keep telling myself that 'it is well with my soul' just like the old hymn says. You know, it was so hard to follow what all of you said, but I *decided* to try." She related to me that it was those very basic steps of singing, saying thank you to God, and staying in church that turned her around. Those things didn't solve it all right away, but she took steps toward her season of change. These simple *decisions* brought her back to God until she realized she had no other choice but to trust Jesus again and decided that her day of change had come.

Today she is one of the most determined prayer warriors in our ministry. Nothing stands in her way. I tell you the truth, hell fears to see her coming! If you need a healing, she is determined that you get healed. If you need prayer, you'll get a slam-bang, throne-room explosion from her. She looks so beautiful, her face shines with the glory of God, and she'll tell you this today, "You don't need God to give you all the answers; you just need to love God with no conditions. If you will move toward Him, no matter how hard that feels, He will show you that He is always good, and His promises are always true."

When her life was tampered with, this woman could have chosen to stay where she was, but she chose to believe the Lord. Yes, she chose her season of change.

I Am Going to See the King

Nehemiah also had to make his own decision for change. When he received the bad report about his friends back home, he couldn't live the rest of his life being hurt by the pain of it. Yes, the pain was real, places and things from his memories had been lost and destroyed, and his heritage was stolen, but he couldn't go backward. He had to do something immediately, so he decided to see the king (Neh. 2:1–8). He went straight to the top for help! This holds a prophetic analogy for us: when you're in trouble, go to the King!

Realistically, Nehemiah had no guarantees that anything good would come from paying the king a visit concerning his problem. After all, the king at that time was Artaxerxes, and he was a Babylonian ruler. He could have had an indifferent ear and been unable to relate to the tragedy in Nehemiah's heart.

You might be saying, "That's right; no one understands what I have been going through. No one has experienced the magnitude of my issue!" One of the greatest deceptions of the devil is to make you believe that you are all alone and no one understands you. But that is the farthest thing from the truth. And that lie causes people to leave family, friends, and churches, and thus abort their entire destiny with God. People run away because they think no one cares or can relate to their problem.

> One of the greatest deceptions of the devil is to make you believe that you are all alone and no one understands you. But that is the farthest thing from the truth.

One thing I do when I feel low about something in life is to remind myself that scores of people have gone through so much worse. It helps me see that this situation is conquerable. Remember, everyone's life has been tampered with. Sure, your situation may have some unique elements to it, but be assured that you are not alone. Maybe at the very present moment you aren't in close contact with anyone who completely understands, but be certain that someone out there knows exactly what you are facing.

When you are feeling alone in your endeavor to rise up, begin by remembering Jesus. If Nehemiah could respond to his tragic events by going to the king, we should respond to every trial of our lives by going to our King—Jesus. The Bible says there is not one thing we can experience that He does not relate to the pain: "For we have not an high priest which cannot be touched with the feeling of our infirmities; but was in all points tempted like as we are, yet without sin. Let us therefore come boldly unto the throne of grace, that we may obtain mercy, and find grace to help in time of need" (Heb. 4:15–16). Now, that just about says it all!

Pulling more enlightening revelation from this scripture, however, we see that the Bible says Jesus experienced everything we experience.

No, He might not have had the identical trials you do, but you will find that what He did experience was even worse. He walked through so many things that on examining them you will find your problems are probably mild in comparison. Let's review for a moment just what Jesus suffered, because, if we are not careful, we forget. Read this carefully because I'll bet there are a few you didn't consider.

First of all, Jesus suffered the loss of a loved one, His dear cousin, John the Baptist (Matt. 14:1–13). Jesus came from what many would consider a dysfunctional family, and, without a doubt, there were rumors somewhere that His mother had been pregnant outside of marriage! You know, news flies through the old hometown. Jesus walked through the betrayal by a friend named Judas (Mark 3:19). His money was stolen by that same friend, Judas, who was His treasurer (John 12:6). He faced the Jerusalem IRS of the day and was required to come up with tax money (Matt. 17:24–27). He was discredited by His own family and friends as a madman (Mark 3:21). He was cast out as a deceiver by the church of the day, called the synagogue (Luke 4:28–29). He knew what it meant to be alone and sorely tempted to sin for forty days straight, during a time when He was weak from hunger (Matt. 4:2–11). He experienced dangerous weather elements serious enough to sink a ship (Mark 4:35–38).

Jesus worked long, exhausting hours on His job of ministry. He would rise early to pray, travel for miles, preach and pray for people all day, and then still find the energy to spend time with God at night. Jesus was lied about so viciously that false stories about Him spread like wildfire around the region. He even had death threats on His life from some very influential people in the community. In fact, they regularly plotted on how to take Him out, like the plotting of modern-day terrorism. Most people have never faced that extreme level of hatred. I would have to say Jesus even understood the threat of gang violence and organized crime. Additionally, people severely laughed at Jesus on a regular basis (Mark 5:40). Of course, this is just a partial list of what He lived through on Earth, but it doesn't end there.

If what Jesus experienced during His thirty-three years on Earth was not enough, when the process of His crucifixion began, He was also tortured and abused. He was beaten so severely before going to the cross that He was barely recognizable as human. Some historical accounts state that He was hung on the cross completely naked. He was spit upon, had His beard torn out, and was slapped and punched in the face (Matt. 26:67–68). Then they ridiculed Him while they beat Him. Now, I think that is the ultimate in humiliation. This proves Jesus knows how it feels to be abused, mocked, and degraded. He also understands the paralyzing hurt of being in physical pain.

> Jesus knows what it means to love and forgive someone, even when they don't always recognize or appreciate the effort.

Remember another point: Jesus was also the victim of someone else's wrongdoing—yours and mine! He became the victim of our sins, and the Bible says He also accepted all the turmoil that came with them (1 Pet. 2:24). So, not only did He manage to overcome His own trials, but He also allowed Himself to be weighted down with our stuff too. Have you ever had to deal with your own problems and then, at the same time, help someone else with theirs? Remember how it weighted you down beyond measure? Jesus knows all about that.

In adding one more thing to the list, Jesus also knows what it means to love and forgive someone, even when they don't always recognize or appreciate the effort. He gave up His glorious place in heaven to come to Earth and love people who didn't really care.

Since I am sure we are now convinced that Jesus can relate to our situations, having had His own experiences, I want to bring out another aspect of His suffering that you may have yet to consider. Have you ever paused to think that because Jesus is God, He knows and sees everything? From before the beginning of this earth He has seen every detail of existence. (See John 8.) That means He has witnessed every murder, every rape, every lie, and every betrayal from Earth's beginning until now. That is a lot of bad stuff. He has heard the cry of every abducted child and seen every aching heart. Then, seeing all the countless wars, acts of occultism, tyrannies, accidents, death, and evil, Jesus has never once lost His joy or His ability to stand and govern the earth. He never quits loving people and seeing a positive future. No wonder the Bible says about Him, "But unto the Son he saith, Thy throne, O God, is for ever and ever: a sceptre of righteousness is the sceptre of thy kingdom" (Heb. 1:8).

I'm telling you, God saw what Jesus pulled off and handed Him the heavenly scepter of rule and called Him God! He is so mighty! I think you will agree that not one human being has ever faced what Jesus faced, nor could we ever hope to even come close and still continue living. Now you can start seeing that your problem is not impossible to defeat.

Be assured, Jesus knows what you have dealt with in life, and He knows just how to bring you out of it. He will teach you how to do it just the way He did—through faith and the anointing of God. He wants to bring you out of the captivity of Babylon, but He wants you to keep your joy and let Him walk you through the process, bringing you into your new place of Zion. Believe me, having been through it all, He *knows* exactly what He is doing. We just need to believe Him.

> Seeing then that we have a great high priest, that is passed into the heavens, Jesus the Son of God, let us hold fast our profession. For we have not an high priest which cannot be touched with the feeling of our infirmities; but was in all points tempted like as we are, yet without sin. Let us

therefore come boldly unto the throne of grace, that we
may obtain mercy, and find grace to help in time of need.
—HEBREWS 4:14–16

This scripture tells us that Jesus understands your problem and
that you can come boldly to His kingly throne. In other words, come
confidently into the King's courtroom and expect that He will hear
and relate to you. Don't go in there complaining, but go as Nehemiah did when he went in expecting a miracle. Even if what you are
dealing with today has you stumped on how you should even pray,
then go boldly and talk with the Lord about that—not rudely, but
with assurance.

"Let us all come forward and draw near with true (honest and
sincere) hearts in unqualified assurance and absolute conviction
engendered by faith (by that leaning of the entire human personality on God in absolute trust and confidence in His power, wisdom,
and goodness)..." (Heb. 10:22, AMP). In a nutshell, when you're in
trouble, don't run from God; run *to* Him! He knows what you are
going through. He knows how you are feeling. Go to your King and
watch what He can do for you!

Prepare for Change Today

If you are going to visit the King about your situation, then make sure
you are prepared to receive the answer. Sometimes we pray things and
live as if the answer isn't coming for another decade. Years ago, during
some of our greatest years of financial struggle, we were visiting the
King about many things. Nevertheless, we were obeying God with
our tithes and finding every way we could to sow other financial seeds.
We were declaring the answer and expecting miracles. Basically we
were doing everything we knew how to do. Back then we had to use
our faith to believe for our basic groceries. I'm sure you can identify
with that too.

One day while I was at home, I received a phone call from someone we knew who said they had some food for us. Now, to my knowledge we had never told this person how much we were standing on God's promises for our daily needs. This person lived on a farm and proceeded to tell me that they had two large coolers of beef to bring us from a cow they had butchered. Then he asked, "When can I stop by?"

> If you are going to visit the King about your situation, then make sure you are prepared to receive the answer.

Now I almost did something completely idiotic. I almost said, "We don't have a place to put that much meat because we only have the little freezer in our refrigerator and there is a lot of ice in it." Can you believe it? That is what captivity will do to you! You won't see the blessing because of the chains!

Man, did I almost flub that one up! I actually began to make excuses on the phone with this person about how I couldn't fit the food in the freezer! So he said to me, "Doesn't the Bible say that you will receive blessings that you won't have room to receive?" (See Malachi 3:10.)

I replied, "Well, yes, it does."

This person continued by saying, "Then you had better start making some room in that freezer because I am on my way." There was so much meat we had to go and get another freezer to hold it all. We had to use a credit card to buy the freezer because, at the time, we didn't have enough cash to get one. But the meat in that freezer fed our family for a long time, and more than once someone blessed us with a side of beef to fill it.

Here we had been praying for months about breakthrough and provision, but when it came, we weren't prepared for it and almost refused it! If you are going to step into your season of change, you have to start preparing right now. If you are expecting God to provide you with some new clothes, then you need to get some of your current ones out of the closet to make space. If you are praying for a new car, then clean the garage out so you have a place to park it! Live like your season of change is coming today, not someday!

Nehemiah had a "today" attitude. When he could have just hoped, he sprung into action. While he was making plans to visit the king, he prayed a "today" prayer. In Nehemiah 1:11 he said, "...Prosper, I pray thee, thy servant this day...."

> If you are going to step into your season of change, you have to start preparing right now. Live like your season of change is coming today, not someday!

What day did he expect God to prosper him? He expected it "this day"—today. As a result, he developed a plan to prepare for it.

Sometimes we wait for God to reveal His plan to us through some spectacular method. And yes, sometimes that is how God will do it. Nehemiah prayed, however, and *immediately* developed a game plan. We don't have any record that God even told him what to do. Although God will give you instructions, and you have to be sensitive to hear and wait for them, you can't have a do-nothing mind-set. If you pray and commit yourself to do the will of God, then God will guide you as you step out and make a move by faith—believing He will provide. It means doing something today that prepares you to step into your season of change.

Notice that Nehemiah came to the king and presented a plan. He took initiative. He asked for the king's support and requested that he be granted a release to go rebuild what was torn down (Neh. 2). As you are waiting for your miracle, don't just pray and wait for someday to come. Start planning like your season of change is now. That does not mean you have to go to drastic measures, like moving across the country. What it does mean is that you take an honest look at what you can be doing to prepare yourself for something new. It may be as simple as buying a freezer!

If you are expecting financial breakthrough, then a good place to start is by learning some basic financial-management skills. Learn to balance your checking account properly, and start making sure you tithe and give offerings. That is a simple way to show the Lord that you are preparing today for your season of change.

Remember the story in 2 Kings 7 that told about the four lepers? There was a terrible famine on the land, and they were hungry. Obviously, being lepers, they were outside the city, but knowing there was a famine and they were going to die in their condition, they made a game plan. They stated the famous words, "Why sit we here until we die?" (v. 3). In other words, they decided that if they just stayed outside the city and did nothing, they would die from hunger for sure. If they would do something about their situation right now, they might stumble upon something to eat. In their plan they decided the only food anywhere was in the camp of the Syrians. Going there was a risk because the Syrian army could have instantly killed these outcast lepers. But they reasoned that they would die anyway, so they went.

Notice they didn't wait around. The Bible says they went that same day as soon as the sun went down (v. 5). They didn't wait for tomorrow; they decided today was their day to get a meal. Powerfully enough, when they got to the camp, it was deserted because the Lord had tricked the Syrian army into thinking they were being pursued by an enemy. So the lepers helped themselves to the food and treasures that the Syrians had left behind when they fled. Then one of the lepers made a powerful statement. He said, "...This is a day of good news..." (v. 9, NLT).

Now what would have happened if they had sat in the desert and just hoped for a miracle? Instead, they got up that very day and went looking for some good news—and found it. Not only did their decision to prepare for change sustain them, but it was also the very breakthrough the king of Samaria needed to stop the famine. When the lepers told the king about the camp, he took horses and captured the tents of the Syrians. Deciding your season of change will not only bless you but also will likely be the answer to prayer for someone else!

Like the four lepers, we need to go looking for some good news rather than just rehearsing what has already happened. When people have experienced a lot of pain and turmoil, they often prepare for the worst to keep happening. That is why so many people live in fear of potential tragedy or illness. Our culture teaches us to prepare for the worst. That is what insurance is all about—planning for a bad day.

Now I am not saying you shouldn't have insurance or save money and all those kinds of things. We live in a world of tribulation where the devil tries to attack and afflict us. Therefore we should be good stewards with our resources so we can stand in the day of evil. Don't live with the mentality, however, that you are "preparing for the worst" all the time. Like those lepers, start looking for the day of good news—start preparing for the best. That is how you get prepared for your season of change.

The Broccoli Is Gone

A number of years ago, we bought a house that already had a little garden plot out back because the previous owner was raised on a farm and did quite a bit of gardening. I was so excited to try it. My parents had a few gardens when I was growing up, and so I thought it would be easy. Since we moved in during the summer months, we didn't have time to plant a garden the first year, but I had made big plans for the next summer. You see, I like to cook. I enjoy a little time of solitude while creating food in the kitchen at the end of a busy workday.

And I had all kinds of ideas about how a garden was going to enhance my cooking experience.

The first day we went out to survey the ground and prepare it for planting, it was about ninety-five degrees. By this time, the ground was as hard as a rock and covered with weeds. My husband responded to the situation by saying, "I don't want to do this, and I think we should forget it."

My answer, "No way," and I was determined! Never get in the way of a determined woman, as most husbands will agree. For the man, a determined woman on a project always translates into work, and lots of it. Anyway, he wanted to wait for a cooler day, but that was not going to work for me. I wanted a garden and I wanted one now.

So we got the shovels and started digging. I mean, it felt like we were trying to dig the Grand Canyon. I had always pictured this dirt like you see on television, all moist and dark brown where you can easily run your hands through it and let it fall through your fingers. That is not what we had. After one small section of digging, about four feet by four feet, we only had large shovel-sized clumps with grass and weeds sticking out all over them. It was horrible. My husband went in and left me to work it alone. Looking back, I don't blame him, but when a woman is determined, look out.

I stayed with it for a while, but after a few hours of sunburn, I had to quit. My husband called someone in our church who informed us that we could rent a tiller. Of course, we didn't know how to use such a thing because in our house we are the sort of people who can't even hang a towel rack. So we found someone who was kind enough to till the ground for us.

Do you realize that preparing the ground for a growing season is the most difficult part? That is where all the resistance is. This is why so many people throw down their shovel and move on to something else. Change is hard sometimes. It isn't easy to own a brand-new car when you have been driving a rust bucket for the last ten years.

Suddenly with a new car you have a potential monthly payment, you need insurance (sometimes lots of it), you have to pay the taxes and the upkeep on it, you have to think about good parking spots so that someone doesn't hit it, and you have to make time to wash and shine it every weekend. With the old car you didn't care where you parked it, what was spilled in it, or how clean it looked. Changing into the new comes with new responsibilities. It's those first steps of change that could make you run back to Babylon where life was *easier.*

Now our garden was ready for planting. I tried planting seeds in those little pots in the house. You know, the little peat pots. I decided seeds were cheaper than plants that were already growing, so to be frugal, I opted for seeds. Nothing grew. After weeks of still nothing growing and our planting season passing us by, I dumped the peat pots in the trash and went and bought the starter plants.

> Changing into the new comes with new responsibilities. It's those first steps of change that could make you run back to Babylon where life was *easier.*

We were still excited about our garden, so we bought everything. I mean, we bought carrots, green peppers, broccoli, radishes, melons, and onions. If you could garden it, we bought and planted it. I even put a couple of carnation plants in there because I thought it would be a nice addition. We put little name stickers by the plants, and we cared for them and nursed them. Do you know they started to grow and vegetables started to appear? We were thrilled. I couldn't wait for my first harvest. For the first time, I actually saw how broccoli looks as it grows on the plant.

Then one morning we went out to check on how our little garden was coming along and received a shock. We couldn't believe our eyes. Every plant except one or two had been eaten by rabbits. The rabbits even bit the tops off the carnations! Our beautiful garden had become a salad even before we harvested it. We only managed to salvage some green peppers and a few tomatoes. The broccoli stems that we were so excited about were completely gone. Needless to say, that morning ended our love of gardening. It was the first and last year we used that old garden space.

The next year we planted it, all right—we planted grass seed! At this point, we didn't care to research how to defend it against pests, rabbits, or playing children. We didn't care about our growing season the following year at all. From then on our garden was located in the produce aisle at the store.

When you come out of the past, your initial steps into change will be the most shocking and challenging because you have learned how to live a different way. A season of change will press on your walk with God, it will challenge your resolve, and it will be the greatest part of warfare. Habits and demons of the past don't easily give up their territory. They are like those clumps of dirt that don't want to be turned over.

As a result, so many people go back to Babylonian captivity because getting ready for a new way of life can stretch you to your limits, even though you know there is a great blessing behind it. A lot of Christians would rather do without a breakthrough than to have to fight for one.

If you want to leave behind whatever trial or problem is troubling you, however, then you must decide your season of change and be willing to stand for it until change comes. It's time to shake yourself from the dust and say, "This is it! Today is my season of change."

And Nebuchadnezzar king of Babylon came against the city, and his servants did besiege it.

[2 KINGS 24:11]

CHAPTER 3

FREEDOM FROM CAPTIVITY

Y OU CAN ALMOST HEAR THE SOUND OF THE HOOVES vibrating the earth beneath them while you picture a band of horses thundering across the countryside toward the Holy City. Jerusalem, the city of peace, was about to be forever changed. As people went about their daily activities, they probably had little idea about what was just around the corner, the tragedy that would bring them into extreme turmoil and despair. It must have felt similar on the morning of September 11, when the people of New York and the rest of America began their normal routines. Nothing seemed out of the ordinary until one moment in time turned the world upside down. Their lives and those of their children were never going to be the same. The city of Jerusalem was about to be destroyed.

Now, this was not just any attack; this was an assault on the people of God by one of the most treacherous kings in Bible history—Nebuchadnezzar, king of the most magnificent city Babylon—and staged in the great Babylonian empire. He was the figure of strength and fear across the territory, a ruthless military leader who stopped at nothing to punish rebellious people who didn't bow to his wishes. He didn't flinch at any method of torture, regardless of the victim. His heart was dedicated to the worship of the god Marduk, and he built a vast pagan temple in Marduk's honor. This king feasted on pride and conquered territories, and he brought Babylon back into her former years of glory.

This siege spoken of in 2 Kings 24 was not King Nebuchadnezzar's only invasion of Judah. He had come in a series of attacks over the previous twelve years, each time deporting numerous Jews back to Babylonia. Probably the most horrific day, however, was in August of 586 B.C. when he smashed through the walls of Jerusalem, destroying all the beloved places of the city—including the precious holy place, the temple of the Lord. He afflicted the people, stole treasures from the temple, and set the city on fire. Imagine the events as all that the people had ever known and loved was lost. Now their children were to be exiles in a land of captivity, pagan worship, and bondage—except for a few of them he left behind to struggle in the ruins under the watchful eye of a governor placed there to enforce their loyalty to Babylon.

I am sure you already recognize the wicked spirit behind Nebuchadnezzar. Doesn't it sound familiar to Babylon's original founder, Nimrod? God's people were about to know firsthand what it means to live under the control of the world. It was going to become their way of life, and everything they did would have to adapt to the secular culture. No longer could they worship the living God in the temple court. Instead they would be expected to bow to the idols of King Nebuchadnezzar's pagan religion. This was to become the only way of life their children would ever know—the way of Babylon, the way of the world.

When individuals have lived under a particular circumstance for a very long time, they form mind-sets. They become accustomed to certain things that after a while they consider normal and acceptable, even if they are terribly wrong. For example, have you ever made a New Year's resolution? You are determined to turn over a new leaf, but after a little while, your past habits come back to haunt you. They speak to you. It's not until the day you decide to give up potato chips that your mouth starts to water for every flavor that is made. Then it gets so bad you decide to go ahead and get some, only to find yourself eating the entire bag. Now, for me it's potato chips and french fries, and I enjoy every delicious bite. For you it might be something else, but reality is your flesh wants to stay in Babylon even when Babylon is killing you! After a while the culture of the world becomes your culture. Even in the kingdom of God, we have to learn how to change our previous cultural mind-sets if we want deliverance from a spirit of captivity.

Since Nebuchadnezzar was the king who conquered the people and brought them into bondage, he would also become the figure that represented captivity to the people. His repeated assaults on their lives were forming a pattern inside them. It was a pattern of terror, torment, and worthlessness, and it probably kept them from having any real goals for the future. Nebuchadnezzar is a picture of the spirit of captivity. A spirit of captivity immobilizes you through the use of trials, experiences, and events.

Someone once coined the famous phrase, "Experience is the best teacher." That can be true, but the problem is that experience can also teach you the wrong things. A person who is severely bitten by a dog, even if it was only once, usually ends up not becoming an avid dog lover. People can have all sorts of fears and phobias because of one bad dream, accident, or tragic event in their lives. Sometimes it is a series of attacks, as it was for the people

> Even in the kingdom of God, we have to learn how to change our previous cultural mind-sets if we want deliverance from a spirit of captivity.

57

when Nebuchadnezzar kept invading them. I know Christians who have prayed about something, and when the answer didn't manifest the way they expected, they were fearful to step out and trust God in a similar way again. They may be fine in other areas, but that one thing still holds them back. Some have prayed for a healing miracle but then watched someone they love die anyway.

When something like that happens, the tendency is to become forever hindered in that particular area of our lives. Then we find ourselves changing the truth of the Bible, God's Word, and His ways to match up with our personal "experiences." This can be easy to do without even realizing we are doing it. That is what captivity will do. I call it the "spirit of Nebuchadnezzar," or simply the spirit of captivity. It is when culture or experience teaches you one thing that is completely different from the ways of the Spirit of God.

Once an area of captivity has taken root in your life, you will start to lose your sense of purpose. Now this may not affect your entire life's purpose—even though for many people it can be that severe. It might be as simple as the fear of flying on an airplane to a life completely inundated by anger and abuse. There are many Christians whose lives are tampered with by a severe spirit of captivity. They love God with all their hearts, but their past was so dysfunctional and full of hurt that now they cannot seem to break out of some horrible habits developed by the past. Even after evil spirits are cast out of them, their minds have to be renewed. In other words, they have to learn a new way of living that is according to God's ways.

For example, if your pattern growing up was that your father could never seem to keep a good job or provide a stable income, then, without realizing it, those years in "Babylon" can lead to a blueprint of similar inconsistency in you. You find yourself going through the years not being able to get ahead in life and thus feeling like a failure without any solid goals to reach. This is how a spirit of captivity tries to destroy your purpose. You have learned something that is not in line with godliness. The demons may have come and gone, but they have already done their dirty work by leaving a permanent imprint on you.

Romans 12:1–2 gives us insight into this revelation and provides some hands-on ways we can change these mind-sets: "I beseech you therefore, brethren, by the mercies of God, that ye present your bodies a living sacrifice, holy, acceptable unto God, which is your reasonable service. And be not conformed to this world: but be ye transformed by the renewing of your mind, that ye may prove what is that good, and acceptable, and perfect, will of God." First, Paul pleads that we should make the serious decision to keep our flesh pure. Whatever your flesh has been used to doing, you must take charge and tell it, "No." This could be a serious addiction, or it could be a bad habit of gossip. It might be the excessive need for constant attention or bad spending habits. According to this verse, it is the least we can do for the Lord.

> Once an area of captivity has taken root in your life, you will start to lose your sense of purpose.

You might be saying, "I want to present myself holy and not give my flesh what it is used to, but I can't seem to stay consistent." Verse 2 offers some further help for us. It tells us not to be conformed to the world. That means you decide not to play the world's game. You realize that God has a different pattern and that you need to learn how to live by it. That is what it means to be transformed. You can cast out the demons, but your mind must change what it has felt secure believing and gravitating toward. The New Living Translation says it this way: "*...let God transform you into a new person by changing the way you think.* Then you will learn to know God's will for you, which is good and pleasing and perfect" (v. 2, emphasis added). There must be a process of renewing when you have been captive to something.

After the chains are broken, you must absolutely relearn how to live. It may mean you are in the "school of the spirit" for a season, learning new mind-sets in one area or another because your mind must be rehabilitated. If all you ever knew growing up was drug and alcohol abuse, when you come out of that abusive lifestyle you are required to form a new pattern. Then the next time you are pressed with a trial or the devil beats you down, you don't revert back into the captivity of addiction. Instead, you are armed with a new and tested source of dependency—God's will and His ways. Your mind has new "experiences" that it can refer to that have replaced your previous ones. This becomes a dependable weapon during times when our lives get tampered with by the devil.

The Stinky-Meat Day

A number of years ago, we received a side of beef as a gift. (This was another side of beef, different from the first one that I spoke of earlier and that originally caused us to buy the freezer.) This side of beef completely filled our freezer. We had been having some work done in our garage, and just after the workers finished, we headed out of town on a short trip for several days. We returned home with our children, only to pull into the garage and be met with the most horrible smell we have ever encountered. It was so bad that we smelled it outside before we even entered the garage.

Once inside the garage, we saw a large pool of red liquid on the garage floor. It was blood! Our minds racing, we didn't know what had happened, until we realized the blood was coming from the freezer. We thought, "No, no, it can't be!" The initial realization of what was happening was paralyzing, not to mention a bit creepy when you come home and see a pool of blood. Something within you wants to start screaming and uncontrollably freaking out. Your mind tries to sort out, "OK, what to do, what to do!"

To top it off, one of our sons was just a two-week-old newborn. So my protective husband immediately grabbed the baby, his carrier, our bags, and me and threw us into the house. We were all heaving from the unbelievable smell. Even our neighbors had begun to smell it!

What happened was that one of the workers at our house had unplugged the freezer to plug in some power tools. After he was finished, he forgot to plug the freezer back into the wall. He didn't know it was the freezer plug. But it was summer, and that entire side of beef had been rotting in the garage for days. I am talking about pounds and pounds of beef. It was so bad we had to call for help. My husband and another friend of our family spent hours cleaning up rotten meat and blood. It was like having a cow butchered right in the garage.

> Even as a Christian, captivity can exist in your life because of the past, or it can try to surface through new trials.

Now, here's what that little event created. Even though they used every imaginable disinfectant, we had trouble ridding the garage of that smell. The freezer was actually salvageable. They were able to take it apart, hose it down, and bleach the whole thing. What the blood did to the porous concrete on our garage floor, however, lasted for months beyond and even into the following summer. We bleached, we scrubbed, and we sprayed things. Then that smell would come back again and again. Each time we came home to…the smell.

After a long busy day at the office, we found ourselves tearing the garage apart trying to defeat the odor. It was imprinted in our senses. We even went to sleep smelling it. Better said, we were "captives" to it.

Captivity will keep coming back to afflict you like that. Second Kings 24:1 says, "Nebuchadnezzar king of Babylon came up..." His evil spirit came upon them, and, historically, he did it repeatedly. One of the main characteristics of captivity is that it keeps coming up again and again. You pray, get in the prayer line, and hate those areas of your life, but when a "hot" day comes, just like the day with our freezer, the smell of it tries to return again.

The devil doesn't play fair, and he will make sure a "hot" day comes to your house. Then, if you are not careful, you start ignoring the smell of it and instead use a "different door into the house" in order to avoid facing it. It is because the roots of certain things run so deep that you don't even remember how they got planted there. Many years after King Nebuchadnezzar was gone and replaced by other Babylonian kings, the effects of what he caused were still in full force. The people's experience with him changed their entire mind-set and culture until they knew nothing else. In fact, those effects lasted and were felt by people who weren't even alive when he was king!

Even as a Christian, captivity can exist in your life because of the past, or it can try to surface through new trials. God wants to deliver us from the roots of captivity in our lives, no matter how large or small. This begins with exposing the operation of this "spirit of Nebuchadnezzar." You might have to ask yourself, "What is my 'Nebuchadnezzar'? What things are hindering my prosperous future and keeping me beat down?"

Captivity in some places can be difficult to detect. But if we understand how it operates, we can expose the hidden places of this "Nebuchadnezzar spirit of captivity" that wants to keep tampering with our lives.

Nebuchadnezzar Exposed

The Bible records several different things that Nebuchadnezzar did to the people. Have you ever had an event happen in your life and it was easy to relive the moment over and over? Without question, this evil king's deeds were seared on the people's minds. Every day was as if they had just lived it yesterday. Well, to understand what God's people had to overcome in order to rise up from their captivity, we need to see what their memory kept reliving. First, there were five specific things he stole from the people. They represent a prophetic picture of what this spirit takes from us. As you read them, think of things that captivity of the enemy has stolen from your life.

Captivity steals your *identity*.

Nebuchadnezzar took the king and the king's family (2 Kings 24:12, 15). This represents their identity as citizens. No longer did they feel a sense of citizenship without a king and a real kingdom to bond to. Captivity keeps God's people from fitting in with the rest of the family of God or seeing themselves as an integral part in the kingdom. In Ephesians 3, Paul prayed for us by saying, "May Christ through your faith [actually] dwell (settle down, abide, make His permanent home) in your hearts! May you be rooted deep in love and founded securely on love, that you may have the power and be strong to apprehend and grasp with all the saints [God's devoted people, the experience of that love] what is the breadth and length and height and depth [of it]" (vv. 17–18, AMP). God wants you to know you are His child and you fit in with the rest of His family. Nebuchadnezzar also took the king in the eighth year of his reign, eight being the number of covenant. When you lose your place and feel like you don't fit in anywhere in God's kingdom, you break covenant and become a captive because you feel like you are an outcast.

Captivity steals your *anointing.*

Nebuchadnezzar stole the precious treasure from the Lord's house and cut the vessels of worship into pieces (2 Kings 24:13). What is the true treasure of the Lord's house? It is the anointing and presence of God. When you lose the precious anointing, you stop sensing God's presence. Your focus toward God feels broken, and you lose your ability to worship freely and intimately. Even when you attempt to worship, it feels empty and dry, and your mind goes back to your problem.

Captivity steals your *vision.*

Nebuchadnezzar stole the leaders and businessmen (v. 14). Without a sense of leadership and direction, you lose your sense of purpose in life. You find yourself wandering from one thing to another, trying to find satisfaction. You don't have any long-term goals, vision, or confidence in your talents. You quit using your talents to do anything significant, and now your struggles have become larger than your goals.

Captivity steals your *authority.*

Nebuchadnezzar stole the mighty warriors (v. 16). This obviously speaks of our authority and warfare. Have you ever been through something where even though you knew what to do, you felt powerless to do it? When your warfare is taken away, you know that a spirit of captivity is at work. You are paralyzed by certain events and reminded of all the times you have failed before. Now you determine there is no point in trying to overcome this issue in your life because you will probably fail again. You see yourself as an inadequate warrior with little anointing to stand victorious against evil forces.

Captivity steals your *confidence*.

Nebuchadnezzar also captured the workers and the craftsmen (v. 16). When captivity is trying to steal your destiny, you will always feel like you can't finish anything, so you withdraw and try to escape. You become apologetic and unsure of yourself. You compare yourself with how everyone else seems to be walking in all that seems to escape you. Someone else always seems to get the job before you. Someone else seems to receive recognition before you, and so on. Every time you venture into something new, there you sit with no fruit to show for it. Captivity keeps you from finishing or feeling good about anything you start because of the insecurity that causes a desire to escape.

Results of Captivity

Now that you have seen what the "spirit of Nebuchadnezzar" steals from you, let's look further at what kind of condition this spirit leaves you in.

Captivity leaves you *surrounded*.

Nebuchadnezzar built forts around the people (2 Kings 25:1). Have you ever felt like you couldn't see a way out because there were too many problems to handle? When captivity tries to take all that God has imparted into your life, you stand there feeling surrounded by the circumstances as if there are just too many things to handle. Captivity will always leave you overwhelmed.

Captivity leaves you *empty*.

Nebuchadnezzar left God's people without bread and in a famine (v. 3). This is when you feel like you cannot locate a fresh word or direction from the Lord. You experience a famine for the Word of the Lord (Amos 8:11). It is almost as if there is some sort of blinder over your spiritual insight. You don't know what scripture to read or even how to begin in prayer. You feel like there is no fresh revelation that applies to what you are facing, and you feel hungry for something from the Lord. You become desperate for a word, a prophecy, a dream, or a scripture that jumps off the pages.

Captivity leaves you *intimidated*.

The people of Jerusalem were running and responded in fear and terror (2 Kings 25:4). This is when you run from your problems because you are too intimidated to address them. You would rather move across the country than face the music where you are. Not only do you run from problems, but you are also always looking over your shoulder "just in case." Some people are captive to various fears, and instead of addressing a problem as a fear, they create unusual remedies. For example, fear of tragic diseases plagues many in our modern day. We have a pill or vitamin for everything. I know people who have boxes and baskets of them—Christian people! But notice how the warriors fled at night. They wanted to run in such a way that they would not be seen by anyone.

People don't want to admit fear, so they try to hide it rather than address it.

Captivity leaves you *confused*.

The people were left scrambling about without any organized plan to follow (v. 5). When you don't have a plan in life and don't know what you are supposed to be doing when you get out of bed tomorrow, then perhaps there is confusion. Confused people are also divisive and disagreeable. They can't seem to get along with anything or anyone because they don't know where they are headed in life. It is dangerous to allow captivity to leave you in confusion because eventually you become full of strife and anger. You become confused and jealous as to why things work for others and not for you. The Bible says, "For where envying and strife is, there is confusion and every evil work" (James 3:16).

Captivity leaves you *blind*.

Nebuchadnezzar put out the king's eyes (2 Kings 25:7). I believe this represents the loss of prophetic insight. It is spiritual blindness that prevents you from seeing God's fresh move and purpose. Then you become bound by formula and religion. You can no longer accurately discern the way of God and thus begin to adopt strange ideas and doctrines. Jesus rebuked the Pharisees for being blind because they had become dead in past religion. They were hypocritical and could not accept the present flow of God. He said they were the blind leading the blind (Matt. 15:12–14). They couldn't see God's prophetic plan and were comfortable in old religion.

Life Without Direction

Now that we have identified the direct characteristics of captivity, we have to know how to get free from it. The one major goal of captivity is to leave you without a real purpose. If the devil can take away your purpose, you won't stand up for anything. Realize that this may not be your lifelong purpose, but it could be a purpose concerning one or two areas in life. It could be because the aim of Nebuchadnezzar is to rob you of your purpose. If the demons of darkness can make that happen, then there is no other battle to fight. They have you.

When you can't see yourself better off in your future and know without a doubt that it is possible to get there with God, then there is nothing left to argue. Above everything else we have to feel a sense of purpose in life no matter how much we have been tampered with. When you have a purpose, you will climb enormous hurdles to fulfill it.

> If the devil can take away your purpose, you won't stand up for anything.

A relative of ours has not been able to locate any sense of purpose in life, and it is reflected in everything she does. Nothing about her has any direction. The characteristics of captivity we just studied have made her devoid of any real stability. She is now getting older and still has no definitive purpose for herself, nor does she have any goals for the future. She has been married more than once, lives on welfare, raised her children with few moral values, has many boyfriends, and has no job. She possesses no real assets and has moved to a new address almost every year or two. She has "committed" her life to Christ several times, even in tears. The problem is that captivity has taken away everything she is, and therefore she walks about without any real purpose in the world, except to find her next rental address and new boyfriend. What a life.

Compare this person somewhat to the children of Judah who lived in Babylon. I am sure there were many like this relative of mine who walked around being bound to Babylon. They were taken there by the dictator Nebuchadnezzar. Dictators always want to leave the people without a purpose because then the people are subjects they can control. If a dictator can make you feel he owns all your stuff, that you don't have an identity; if he keeps you poor, abuses you into submission, and makes you feel like you have no value, then you will do his bidding. Satan is a dictator who wants to steal our purpose and keep us under his control.

So picture the citizens of Judah in Babylon, most of them living in these conditions, not like slaves as in Egypt, but as subjects under foreign rule. They no longer had any ownership or citizenship to claim. Their own land had been invaded and stolen, and they were foreigners in Babylon. Remember Daniel? As a captive subject he wasn't allowed to pray freely; otherwise he would be thrown to the lions (Dan. 6). Then the three captive Hebrew boys were thrown into the furnace for not worshiping Nebuchadnezzar's idol (Dan. 3). Daniel and the three Hebrew children were made to feel they had no identity for which to be proud. In fact, they were even given Babylonian names. It's bad enough to be taken from your own land, but taking a person's name away is the ultimate way to rob them of their sense of purpose in life. To rise above the captive mind-sets, they would have to face some things that they didn't want to face in order to reclaim a sense of identity.

A Whole Lot of Babylon Going On

Realizing the circumstances surrounding the children of Judah living for such a number of years as captives, it makes you appreciate the boldness and confidence of Nehemiah to rise up and go to the king about their heritage being stolen. The people had been invaded, degraded, and overthrown. Even though Nehemiah had favor with the king, coming from captivity and rebuilding their lives was going to be a process.

Surely Nehemiah was well aware of the resistance that Zerubbabel and the children of Judah encountered a few years prior when King Cyrus had released them to rebuild the temple in Jerusalem. They had all kinds of enemies resisting them, even though the king had given them the right to do it. In fact, the temple he allowed them to build didn't even get finished during Cyrus's reign. Ezra 4:24 says, "Then ceased the work of the house of God which is at Jerusalem. So it ceased unto the second year of the reign of Darius king of Persia." The people were beginning to rise from the captivity that Nebuchadnezzar had inflicted years before. They were about to find out, however, that they had many enemies who didn't want them free. They were also about to discover that there was a whole lot of "Nebuchadnezzar's Babylon" intertwined into the people's way of life.

> Jesus has released you from your sins and chains, but He wants to walk you through the process of rebuilding your spiritual house.

When we become Christians and turn our lives over to Jesus, He sets us free from the power of a "Nebuchadnezzar spirit" so we can rebuild our lives as the temples of the living God, just the way King Cyrus did for the children of Judah. Actually, King Cyrus is a prophetic picture of Jesus. God placed His Spirit upon Cyrus to release the captivity of His people. Ezra 1:2 says, "Thus saith Cyrus king of Persia, The LORD God of heaven hath given me all the kingdoms of the earth; and he hath charged me to build him an house at Jerusalem, which is in Judah."

Jesus has released you from your sins and chains, but He wants to walk you through the process of rebuilding your spiritual house. That means in the process of coming out of your past captivity you will encounter some enemies. Next you will probably find, just as the children of Judah did, that you have a whole lot of Babylon going on!

The experience of the children of Judah rising from captivity is much like our own. As we talk about their experience, I want you to imagine yours. Throughout Ezra 1–8, they experienced unbelievable warfare. Everything seemed to be going great, and the temple was finally finished. They began returning the gold vessels that had been taken and putting them back into the house of the Lord. People were celebrating their victory until...until what? This couldn't be true! Ezra couldn't believe his ears. Here God had mightily begun to restore them as a people, they had overcome countless attacks, and now this. Ezra 9:1–2 explains it this way: "Now when these things were done [the completion of the temple], the princes came to me, saying, The people of Israel, and the priests, and the Levites, have not separated themselves from the people of the lands, doing according to their abominations....For they have taken of their daughters for themselves, and for their sons: so that the holy seed have mingled themselves with the people of those lands."

Wow! Even though they were free from captivity through the help of Cyrus, they still had some issues. Little did they know that their lives had become somewhat comfortable with Babylon. They were used to it by now and had learned how to mingle and fit in with the lifestyle. They married some of the citizens and had children who were born by them. When Ezra heard the news, he fell into despair. Notice he didn't say, "Well, that's OK; we all have some vices. Just do your best to live for God."

No, he tore his clothes, pulled his hair out, and cried (Ezra 9:3). He realized how permanent this captivity had become. His reaction is written about in Ezra 9:4 using these words: "...and I sat astonied...." He was shocked and horrified at how much the culture of captivity had become the way of life for the people. You would think the past sins that originally made them captives would have been all the lesson they needed. But instead they were learning to accept the ways of the world.

Doesn't this sound like the process we experience after coming out of the world? We want to serve God, but we have become used to Nebuchadnezzar's invasion. We have learned to accept it until we marry its citizens—making commitments and alliances with things that reflect the world. Some of these are control, rejection, anger, jealousy, bitterness, depression, gossip, fear, perversions, and addictions. Some of these are things we don't think are too terrible to do, but they keep us from living in God's best for our lives. Of course these are just a few of the cultures of "Babylon" that we have married. Now Ezra was shocked that these cultures ran that deep in the people of God, even though they had been delivered. They were certainly going to require some training on how to live outside of the Babylonian culture.

> You are the temple of the Lord that Jesus wants to rebuild. He is there to help separate you from the memories and influences of your past and to live inside you to force every bad habit, every bad attitude, and every feeling of failure out of your life.

Place yourself in their shoes for a moment and think of the magnitude of what this entailed. They had married and had children in Babylon. In chapters 9–10, Ezra stood up and told the people they were going to have to make a separation and come out of captivity. He told them they could no longer have wives from that culture. They could no longer hang out with the people they loved. They couldn't accept the cultures they loved. Strange wives for the children of Israel always spoke of a compromised culture. Today we don't literally separate from a spouse we have already married or disown our literal children in order to be pure. What it means to us now is that we separate ourselves from certain cultures of the world that we have grown to love and believe. In some cases it means making some serious decisions.

Nebuchadnezzar Removed

The children of Israel were faced with some serious decisions. They counted the cost, however, and chose to become separate from the only source of comfort many of them had ever known. Think of the incredible choices they were making. Ezra 10:12 says, "Then all the congregation answered and said with a loud voice, As thou hast said, so must we do." They discovered that, unknowingly, the "spirit of Nebuchadnezzar" had formed a way of life in them that they didn't realize was there. Notice they didn't say, "Well, what did you expect, Ezra? We didn't ask to live here, so it's not our fault!" Many people don't remove the influence of Babylon because they feel it's not their fault that they were taken there. Maybe your parents didn't take the proper responsibility in how they raised you. You could use that as an excuse to remain in Babylon for the rest of your life. But to truly be free after your life has been tampered with, you will have to let go of the excuses.

A friend of ours once told us about a time when she was trying to overcome a spirit of anger. She admitted that she had a bit of a temper and one time was feeling badly after a moment of blowing up at someone. Immediately she said, "Well, Lord, I'm sorry. I just can't help it because I'm French and French people have tempers."

She said she then heard the Lord speak loudly inside her and say, "Well, I'm not French!" In other words, the Holy Spirit in you is not focused on why you are a captive. He is interested in bringing you out of the captivity! Someone may have horribly hurt you and left you broken and bruised in life. But God wants you to get past that hurt so it doesn't keep you in bondage, doing things you hate for the remainder of your life. While in captivity, the children of Israel had to take responsibility for it even when, for some, it wasn't their fault they were placed in that culture. Ezra himself repented for allowing captivity to invade them, even though he wasn't the one who actually committed any of those cultural sins (Ezra 9:8–11).

Remember how the people replied to Ezra: "...so must we do" (Ezra 10:12). They decided to remove Nebuchadnezzar's influence from their lives. They began by recognizing the problem and removing it. You are the temple of the Lord that Jesus wants to rebuild, and He is there to help separate you from the memories and influences of your past to make it happen. He has come to live inside you to force every bad habit, every bad attitude, and every feeling of failure out of your life. Praise God for that! Second Corinthians 6:16–17 says, "And what agreement hath the temple of God with idols? for ye are the temple of the living God; as God hath said, I will dwell in them, and walk in them; and I will be their God, and they shall be my people. Wherefore come out from among them, and be ye separate, saith the Lord, and touch not the unclean thing; and I will receive you."

> God can impart miracles that will shake you and change your entire outlook on life in one moment of time.

That is what God is looking for with you. He wants the spirit of captivity removed so there is more room for Him in our lives. The next verse goes on to say, "And [I] will be a Father unto you, and ye shall be my sons and daughters, saith the Lord Almighty" (v. 18). Regardless of the habits and lifestyles you have become accustomed to living in, you will find them losing their influence on you when you see God as your Father. The captive children of Israel once saw Nebuchadnezzar's culture as the figure of control that provided for their needs. They were the offspring of that lifestyle. When you start to see God as your Father—not just in theory, but with a deep revelation—you will naturally become separate from Babylon. You begin to depend on your Father.

My children know the "culture" of our house. They know the kinds of food we normally eat, they definitely aren't afraid to ask for things—especially money—and they are comfortable with our family life. The life of some family down the street is unfamiliar to them because they know their own parents. They are used to our schedules, the smell of our laundry, and the way we all talk during dinner. When you know your heavenly Father, you become unfamiliar with another "family." Your Father wants to be your greatest source of influence and to replace what you once knew. You can ask the Lord to reveal Himself to you as your Father. For many whose lives have been tampered with, this is difficult to do because so many people didn't have a positive fatherly influence in their lives.

Ask the Lord to help you receive Him as the good Father that He is. You don't always have to understand *how* He will do it because the Lord is supernatural. He can impart miracles that will shake you and change your entire outlook on life in one moment of time. God is your Father, and your Papa is not afraid to chase Nebuchadnezzar's bondage away from the children He loves!

So let's review briefly how to begin removing Nebuchadnezzar's captivities from our lives:

Expose the captivity.

Acknowledge what is holding you captive. It may be a type of fear, an attitude, your words, or an addiction. Be willing to see these areas and call them what they are in your life—captivity and bondage. Exposing the roots will make it lose its ability to keep growing back. Face it and then start a new life pointed in another direction.

No more excuses.

Take responsibility for living as a captive. How or why you were invaded by the devil can no longer be your focus. Repent now and get your own actions right before the Lord so you can move on to reclaim your real purpose in life.

Separate from Babylon.

Decide you do not want the spirit of captivity in your life, and be willing to detach from it. The children of Israel had to make the decision to come out of captivity and change their habits. They could not keep going back to what had become familiar. They had to learn a whole new way of living.

Run to your heavenly Father.

When you decide to see God as your Father, all the other control figures in your life will start to weaken as the culture of your new family takes over.

Of course, when you compare the spirit of captivity to the power of God, it begins to look weaker and weaker. If you allow Him to, the Lord will deliver you from any type of past culture this "spirit of Nebuchadnezzar" has imparted to you. That is what Jesus came for—to set you free—and you can know today that He is an expert at doing it.

In your patience possess ye your souls.

[LUKE 21:19]

[CHAPTER 4]

The ENEMIES of the MIND

C HARLOTTE'S HAPPY CHILDHOOD WAS ABOUT TO COME to a screeching halt when she was just eleven years old. Most of her childhood was normal and happy, and she even had a certain childhood relationship with the Lord, doing all the normal things most children do.

Charlotte wanted to be a Christian, but she did not grow up in a Christian home. Then one day all of the happiness she had known was about to be stolen from her life by a deep secret. It was a secret she didn't tell anyone, even her mother, because the secret was about her dad. Suddenly the seemingly normal childhood love she had toward her own father began to be tampered with when he began initiating unusual affection toward her. He began touching her, except something was not right about it. It felt wrong and very dark. It made her feel so dirty and ashamed. For the next four years, her father would begin to repeat cycles of sexually touching and kissing his own daughter.

This young girl went from being a happy, normal child to a child filled with confusion and utter despair. Her own soul was going to carry a wound that would run very deep into her being, more than she would yet know. From this point on, young Charlotte's mind would struggle to understand and recognize real love, especially from men. Her soul was confused and unable to discern true fatherly love.

In deep pain and alone in some nearby woods one day, Charlotte decided to pray. She told the Lord that she was making plans to run away from home. Her intentions were to go to a nearby city, only a few hours away, and become a prostitute. Reasoning within herself, she decided it would be better to be touched by strangers than to have her dad touch her again. She was losing her ability to reason clearly now, and she began to create her own emotional bandages to fix the deep scars left on her heart and soul.

To her surprise, that day she heard God call her name. Out in the woods, she heard God drop these words deep into her broken heart: "You know the devil wants you to turn out badly and become a prostitute because of what has happened to you. He planned this for you. The best way to pay him back is to turn out good!"

To Charlotte, somehow those words made sense. She determined not to be a prostitute because she felt it was the only way she could have revenge on the devil. But there were many years ahead before Charlotte would rise from her pain.

Everything came to a head one day when Charlotte's mother was out of town and her father tried to get her drunk. This time, as her dad began to make these same advances, Charlotte ran and locked herself in her room before he could molest her. She stayed there all night to get away from him. The next morning when she opened the door to her room, her dad came to her crying, sorry for what he had been doing. Of course, unmoved by his tears, Charlotte told him off! She told him that he had to stop doing those awful things to her. Later she said that her words must have had the power of God on them because, even though these episodes had been going on for nearly four years, her dad never touched her inappropriately again.

Charlotte will tell you that she went through a hellish situation, and it would require the power of God entering her life to deliver her from the pain and confusion of it. She walked through deliverance and much emotional healing in the years to follow. After working through years of some very confused emotions about male relationships and the meaning of a loving father, Charlotte still made the effort to serve God with all her heart because she knew she had heard His voice while in the woods that day. She decided that she could not get away from the words God told her. She couldn't blame Him for her trial because she knew it was the devil who was trying to make her turn out badly.

No matter what, the fight inside her was not going to let that happen. Somehow she would fight, and she was determined to win. One by one, through the power of God, she won the battles raging in her own mind because of this one determined belief. She told herself that she was going to turn out good. More than twenty years later, the plan to become a prostitute is only a faint memory. Through His supernatural work, the Lord even began to restore her relationship with her dad and teach her what it truly means to extend the forgiving power of Christ to someone who has hurt you.

I have personally been close to Charlotte for many years. Today, she serves God mightily in her church where she ministers to many people in their own walk with the Lord. She has an impact on many people whose lives have also been tampered with. She definitely turned out good because Charlotte did one amazing thing—she won the battle for her own soul!

The Command Center of Man

Well, if it's the battle for our soul that we need to win, then we had better know what that battle is. Created in the image of God Himself, we are three-part beings. We are spirit beings, we own a soul, and we live in a body. This means that just as God Himself is the Trinity— which is the Father, the Son, and the Holy Spirit (1 John 5:7)—we also possess three attributes that make up a whole person. We are spirit beings just as God is a Spirit (John 4:24).

God is a Spirit—the Holy Spirit. The Holy Spirit is the life, breath, and movement of God. Your spirit is where life comes from too, often referred to in Scriptures as your heart. It is what keeps you breathing and living—not as your physical heartbeat does, but fueled by the God of all life who makes you an eternal being. When a person's spirit leaves their body, that body can no longer live and therefore it dies.

We also have a soul, which is our intellectual mind where we have the ability to reason and discern wisdom. God the Father is represented as the mind of all wisdom and intellect. The Father expresses the will of God (Gal. 1:4). In essence, He is the soul of God, the command center of the Lord. Your soul takes in information and is the command center of your entire being.

> You can have most of your life in order with God, but if just one area is out of whack, it can make you feel like *everything* is going badly.

Next is the body. God's body is Jesus, who came as human flesh (John 1:14). Your body is your physical being—your arms, your legs, your flesh. A person's body must stay healthy to function properly and in connection with their spirit and their soul. If a body becomes too sick to keep functioning, their spirit will leave, and, as I stated previously, that body will die. To live here on this earth we need all three parts of our being working together.

When you became a Christian, your inner man (your spirit) was born again and re-created (2 Cor. 5:17) so it could become clean and able to house God's holy presence. The sins that stained your very life were washed away so that God could make His home in your heart and breathe new life into you. Therefore your soul (your mind and command center) must learn to dictate to the inside of you a new way of living that pleases God. All the previous negative information your soul has taken in from the past must be reprogrammed toward righteousness. It will convert you from making the same ungodly decisions to making godly ones. As your soul begins to receive new information from God and His Word, you slowly begin to act out of a new nature.

Without this process of our souls becoming renewed, we cannot govern ourselves correctly. But once we have our minds, or souls, renewed through God's Word, we will gradually begin to dictate to our bodies and thus change the way we live!

Own Your Soul

Luke 21:19 teaches us one of the most powerful principles in Scripture: "In your patience possess ye your souls." In short, it literally means *to be in control of your own mind.* I believe that if we will grab hold of this truth it will transform every area of our Christian lives from instability to stability. I definitely want stability in every part of my life, don't you?

You can have most of your life in order with God, but if just one area is out of whack, it can make you feel like *everything* is going badly. Do you know what I am talking about? You know your job is great, your finances are working out fine, and you have a great church and a wonderful family. But that relationship with your brother? That's another thing. And it really gets you down. If it weren't for that, you would have a great life.

Your soul is the same way. It could seem that you have an almost normal emotional life, but it's that one thing that gets you. It's that one area of fear that seems to control you, that one little feeling of bitterness or rejection that needles at your walk with God and takes away your joy. Then that very same captivity—that "spirit of Nebuchadnezzar"—comes back to invade again and again. When you can overcome the areas that hold your mind, you will step into a new realm with God.

Another way of interpreting or paraphrasing Luke 21:19 is to say, "With committed endurance be in control of your own mind." It takes a commitment to own your soul, and you must realize that it isn't an overnight process. Life's hurts and disappointments seek to steal the ownership of your mind. They want to fill it with all sorts of painful and negative information. This same information will eventually turn into wrong choices, lack of discernment, and confusion.

"For what is a man profited, if he shall gain the whole world, and lose his own soul? or what shall a man give in exchange for his soul?" (Matt. 16:26). I believe losing your soul is more than just missing out on heaven when you die, which is often the only way we refer to this scripture. We think losing our soul only means going to hell for eternity. I believe, however, the loss of our soul includes even more than that. It also means we give up the ability to govern and be in control of our own minds. We lose our ability to reason correctly or to live by good wisdom. I like the way The Message Bible says it: "What kind of deal is it to get everything you want but lose yourself? What could you ever trade your soul for?" Many people are gradually losing themselves! They are losing themselves to material things, disappointments, problems, and stress. They can no longer remain in possession of their souls. Something else owns their soul, and it's called the weights and captivities of this world.

God wants us to be in complete control of our own minds so we can respond to Him accurately, so we can make sound decisions about our lives, and also, very importantly, so we can victoriously weather the tests and trials life tries to throw at us. You cannot do that if your mind is out of sorts all the time. Think about it: have you ever been really angry about something? When you are very mad, you often forget what's really important at the time. All you can think about is your anger. If you are not careful, you will start doing or saying things you will later regret. You stop governing your life in righteousness and find yourself doing some stupid things.

I cannot emphasize enough that a key to coming back from the dust and ashes that life has left around you is to stay in your right mind. Remember Charlotte's story? She had trouble making sound decisions about her life because she was so severely hurt. A person who is in full control of their mental faculties wouldn't even consider prostitution as a future. It requires a person whose mind and emotional soundness have been compromised.

When your life has been tampered with in some way by the devil, your mind takes in the information, processes it, and then automatically attempts to place it in your memory bank to use as a reference for future decisions about life. For example, if you slipped once stepping into the bathtub, then it is very likely that by the end of the day, you will go to the store to buy some slip guards for the bottom of the tub. Why? It's because your mind banked the information from your experience of slipping in the tub and caused you to make a decision about your future safety. Evil spirits know very well how this works. They will plan circumstances to hurt you in an effort to permanently compromise your ability to respond to certain things in a sound, biblical manner. They know that your mental faculties will bank that negative information for future use, and they're waiting to see you respond to that disappointment or hurt accordingly.

> God wants us to be in complete control of our own minds so we can respond to Him accurately, make sound decisions about our lives, and victoriously weather the tests and trials life tries to throw at us.

There are so many good people alive today who have been tampered with in this way. This is often the reason a woman who was abused in a marriage or a dating relationship will go out and find yet another abusive man. Now, other people in their "right mind"—who haven't been tampered with in that particular area—will throw their hands in the air and ask, "Why in the world would any woman do such a thing? Can't she see it?"

We have all fallen into the same traps in some area or another, and the truth is, we are often the *last ones* to see it. Most people are far less aware of their shortcomings and personality quirks than the people closest to them. Our family and friends can plainly see our flaws! When your life has been tampered with, God wants you to repossess your own soul in whatever way it was compromised. Now, that is usually not a quick-prayer, instantaneous thing. It is a process of receiving God's anointing of power and allowing His Spirit to reprogram your mind about those things. Defeating the enemies that hold our minds in captivity is something every Christian must learn to do effectively. If not, we will have trouble rising from the mark left by some test or trial.

This is why the devil works very hard to win the battleground of your mind. He knows this is your command center and whatever remains in your mind will eventually control your actions. He will use all sorts of deceptive measures to accomplish it. He will try to make you believe that your mind is playing tricks on you and deceive you into responding to lies, overwhelming emotions, and "mental mirages." A few ways the devil will try to work on your head is when you conjure up scenarios about people that are false, when you mull over your own disappointments, or when you are bombarded with various mental fears. God has given us the way of overcoming the war of the mind so that when the devil or people attack us, we can keep our souls under control and walk in peace and godliness.

Knowing Your Soul

To better understand how to win the battle for your soul, it is helpful to know that the soul is divided into five parts, which I will discuss briefly here so you will know how they function. Understanding how your mind works will help you take an active position in keeping it in line with the Lord.

Your will

The will is the most dominant force of the human soul. It has the final say in your decisions. Many people cannot get anywhere in life because they can't possess their souls when it comes to their will. They have trouble making a decision and sticking with it. Solomon had the determination of his will when he built the temple (2 Chron. 2:1). Remember only *you* have power over your own will. The Holy Spirit will not take control of your will; He will only guide and direct it.

This also means the devil has no power over your will either.

> If the simple, daily choices about God are waning, then it's time to pull your will back into focus.

He will, however, use other attributes of your soul to *get at* your will and to get you to give in or give your will over to him. Remember, he deceived the will of Eve by using her memory. He made her question God when he asked, "Hath God said...?" (Gen. 3:1). Then Satan worked on other areas of her soul such as her emotions and feelings.

Be alert regarding your will. When you find yourself making lethargic decisions about godly and spiritual things, you must stir your will back to godliness by double-checking all your decisions about spiritual things. Did you pray today? Are you making the choice to read your Bible and go to church? If the simple, daily choices about

God are waning, then it's time to pull your will back into focus. When it comes to your will, "just do it."

Your emotions

Emotions are biblical and given by God. They are what make us enjoy color and give us personality. Emotions make us unique. Emotions are good, but they need to be governed by God. They can be very powerful and make you easily believe a lie based on a "feeling." That feeling could have been the result of lack of sleep or something a person said to you. Emotions can have such a paralyzing impact that you can easily find yourself responding suddenly and irrationally to them. This is why the devil loves to use our emotions against us. They can affect your entire being and thus are a very powerful attribute of your soul.

> When logic overrides your faith and inward witness of the Holy Spirit, your intellect is under attack.

In a good way, your emotions can help you understand the anger of God and the joy of the Lord, as well as help you recognize when the Holy Spirit is grieved. Emotions should not, however, determine whether you are in God's will, nor should they be used to prove the work of the Holy Spirit.

Carnal emotions are easier to recognize than we think. They will always feel opposite to the principles of the Word of God. For example, you feel anger, but the Scripture clearly says that we must walk in love and forgiveness. Handling your emotions begins by speaking to them and telling them to line up with God's Word, even when you don't "feel" like it.

Your intellect

Your intellect is best described as your mental intelligence that helps you understand wisdom and discretion. This is what we call "using your brain." It is the learning center of your soul and where you gather knowledge and information. It can help you know God, both through revelation and a process of study. When people allow their intellect to be given over to spirits of humanism, they begin to believe they are smarter than God (Rom. 1:22).

The intellect is also what holds many people captive to a religious spirit because they need a logical explanation for everything. When logic overrides your faith and inward witness of the Holy Spirit, your intellect is under attack. "The fear of the LORD is the beginning of wisdom: a good understanding have all they that do his commandments" (Ps. 111:10). This means the way you begin aligning your intellect with God is to fear Him and love Him enough that you want to please Him by keeping His commandments.

Your imagination

A godly imagination has the wonderful ability to create vision. It builds your destiny and dreams for the future. Through the seeds of imagination you can "grow" anything for God. Your imagination must stay submitted to the plans and direction of God. Otherwise you will run out on your own and possibly miss the Lord's best for your life. You know when your good-intentioned imaginations are getting ahead of God because they become tainted by self-exaltation. Isn't that what happened to Lucifer? He said, "I will ascend above the heights of the clouds; I will be like the most High" (Isa. 14:14).

Now, you may not have aspirations to personally outdo God, but you could be trying to outdo other people and covet the praise of man. Once again Satan tricked Eve in the garden. This time it was by using her imagination against her when he said that she could "be like God" (Gen. 3:5, AMP). Instead of wanting to be like the Lord in a pure way, she wanted to "be like God" in a prideful way.

The devil also attacks our imagination through fantasies. The world uses fantasy as an escape from life's pressures. Obviously the entire entertainment industry is rooted in fantasy. But fantasy can taint a pure imagination. The devil will encourage you to fantasize in order to "escape" your trials when, in fact, fantasy is the trap meant to hold you captive to your problem. Of course, there is nothing wrong with clean fun as long as it does not prevent you from facing reality in your life.

Second Timothy 4:3–4 says, "For the time is coming when [people]...will turn aside from hearing the truth and wander off into myths and man-made fictions" (AMP). A proper imagination needs proper ideas and fuel to direct its thoughts. You can keep your imagination in check by starting with humility, then filling your mind with new, godly things to think on. The things that get most of your attention are what you will find yourself daydreaming about through the day.

Your memory

Your memories are the archives of your soul realm. They serve as a reference point for what you do and how you respond, and, if the memories are the right ones, they even help you make sound choices. Good memories and even certain kinds of negative ones will actually help your decision-making process. For example, a child who burns his hand on the stove will have a memory of that painful experience, but it will also remind him to use care near stoves for the rest of his life. Now, God didn't plan for that bad experience, because He doesn't harm us in order to teach us things. Nevertheless, that child's memory will still serve to keep him safer in the future.

Perhaps you remember a "bad experience" at a restaurant. It is more than likely you will never eat there again because your memory will tell you not to go. The devil, however, most often likes to use a bad memory and turn it into fears and phobias. His aim is to keep you captive to a host of bad memories. Many people's lives have been tampered with by demons, and, even as Christians, they live captive to the memories of these events for many years. Then the devil will re-create other scenarios that mimic that bad time in your life and hit you with thoughts that say, "Remember the other time this happened? Remember how badly it hurt you?" Now you are afraid of being hurt again. And it becomes so easy to make decisions and respond to things completely outside of biblical principles and righteousness.

Evil spirits love to use your memories as an access point to keep you captive to the past. They will try to torment you with your memories, even using other people to remind you of those memories and hold them over you. Then you begin attracting the type of people who feed that mental image. Those bad memories will rob you of a good conscience. As you keep looking back on your past hurts, disappointments, and mistakes, rejection can set in. Rejection keeps you feeling bad about yourself and unworthy to accomplish anything for the Lord, even when you are living right and holy for God.

> Whenever God decides to place you in His "school" to learn something, most of the time you aren't even aware that you were enrolled until graduation day.

Command tormenting spirits to leave your memory. You have authority over them in Jesus's name! Then take hold of God's promises concerning your memory, and ask the Lord to remove all ill effects from any bad memories. I believe the supernatural power of God can come upon you and cause the bad memories to completely lose their hold over you. It will be as though it was someone else who walked through those events. Isaiah 43:18–19 says, "Remember ye not the former things, neither consider the things of old. Behold, I will do a new thing; now it shall spring forth; shall ye not know it? I will even make a way in the wilderness, and rivers in the desert." God wants to replace your old memories and give you new and wonderful memories with Him.

Answer Your Enemy

As I shared before, when my husband and I were first married we had many aspirations for our future. Both of us felt called and dedicated to ministry. Preaching and touching people's lives were all we ever wanted to do. Then back in 1989, we received a prophecy from Benny Hinn about our ministry. Not knowing us or ever having met us, he called us out of the audience and said, "'I see you as two fruitful trees walking,' says the Lord, 'and the two of you shall go and bear much fruit in the earth.'" Those words rang in our hearts like a bell! We were ready for our destiny with God. Little did we know that to get to the fruit-bearing part of ministry, it was going to require some tilling of our ground, some seed planting, and some spiritual weed killing.

Thinking we knew everything, we discovered we still had a lot to learn. Through much prayer, study, and life experiences, we began to enter God's ministerial "school of the Spirit." Now, being in the school of the Spirit doesn't mean you become a self-righteous loner who does nothing more than create your own "lessons" and self-made "diplomas." I have found that whenever God decides to place you in His "school" to learn something, most of the time you aren't even aware that you were enrolled until graduation day. Then you say, "Oh, yeah, God, so that's what You were up to!"

Our "school of the Spirit" occurred as we were doing what we knew to serve God, be involved in church and pursue His plan for our lives.

Right out of the gate, however, we got tampered with. Not only were we in the school of the Spirit, but the devil decided to ride along with us too! He wanted to knock us off course at every turn. I believe God only allowed this for one main reason: we had to learn how to answer our enemy. I mean, every discouraging scenario seemed to come our way. We were removed from a religious denomination primarily for preaching that God heals today. We were without an income on many occasions, so we had to trust God for food. We struggled to find a good church, and we definitely didn't have any openings for any full-time ministry in which we could make a decent living. We decided to get secular jobs, and at one point my husband lost his job twice within six months! We lived off credit cards to pay the rent and eat. It felt like a wilderness!

In these situations, your mind starts to tell you things. That's where the real battle is—in your soul! You start to picture the worst happening every time you step out to do something because that is what happened the last time. You know you shouldn't entertain such ideas, so you try to put it out of your mind. But it comes at you again! If you're not careful, you get discouraged and down on yourself, becoming overwhelmed by a sense of failure. I am sure you have had similar situations where you come away from them not knowing what to think. We prayed, fasted, and sowed seed, but much of our circumstances didn't seem to get any better. We wanted so badly to give up on everything! Sometimes we felt angry with God, as if He had deserted us. We felt like we had failed, and we knew some people were laughing at us.

> Before Jesus could walk in His miracle ministry, He first had to learn how to answer His enemy.

Before Jesus could walk in His miracle ministry, He first had to learn how to answer His enemy. The Bible says He was in the wilderness for forty long days of intense spiritual warfare: "And Jesus being full of the Holy Ghost returned from Jordan, and was led by the Spirit into the wilderness, being forty days tempted of the devil. And in those days he did eat nothing" (Luke 4:1–2). So it was far more warfare than just three little temptations—actually, they weren't so little. I have a feeling that Jesus had those three in particular recorded in Scripture because they were the ones that worked the hardest on Him.

Jesus spent forty intense days learning how to answer the devil. Then we read a few verses later, "And Jesus returned in the power of the Spirit..." (v. 14). The reason Jesus was able to return with the full power of the anointing after His test in the wilderness was because He learned how to answer His enemy during that time. Now every time the enemies of His day tried to tamper with His call, His life, and His ministry, He always knew how to answer them.

Have you ever noticed that when the religious leaders tried to question Jesus, He always had a brilliant answer for them? And they walked away stumped. Jesus didn't have to be rude and obnoxious either. He just gave them a straight answer, and He answered His enemies immediately so their verbal attacks could not take root in His mind.

> You have to answer the enemy or he will keep talking to you, and eventually he will talk you into failure.

Learning to answer every enemy that speaks to your mind is the way to win the war of the mind. Nehemiah had to answer his enemies when he began to restore the walls of Jerusalem that Nebuchadnezzar had torn down. When Nehemiah's enemies who did not want the walls rebuilt heard his plans, "They laughed...and said, What is this thing that ye do?" (Neh. 2:19). They spoke to intimidate him. But the Bible says Nehemiah had an answer for them. While they were laughing and resisting him: "*Then answered I them*, and said unto them, The God of heaven, he will prosper us; therefore we his servants will arise and build: but ye have no portion, nor right, nor memorial, in Jerusalem" (Neh. 2:20, emphasis added).

Now, how many times does the devil try to put a thought in your mind that you don't answer? We have all done that far too often. Maybe the devil has told you that you will always be a failure. Maybe thoughts keep screaming in your mind that you will never be free from the captivity of addiction. Perhaps you keep hearing thoughts that you are going to die or that you will never hold down a decent-paying job. Whatever the thought might be, don't just allow it to pass through unanswered. Start talking back to the things that talk to your mind. Notice that Nehemiah told his enemies they had "no right" to what he was doing. Those thoughts have no right to you either, but you have to tell them so! You have to answer the enemy or he will keep talking to you, and eventually he will talk you into failure.

I know a woman whose life fell into despair because she received one thought that she did not answer. As a teenager she served the Lord, and God was doing wonderful things with her family. Then one day her father received military orders, and she and her family had to move. The place they were currently living was the place she became a Spirit-filled Christian; all she loved was there. She was devastated about leaving. Rather a shy person who didn't have a lot of friends, she was very upset at the prospect of having to make new ones, and she started thinking that God was punishing her through this move. (Watch how dangerous one thought can be if you don't know to address it.)

As a result of one deceptive belief that she was being punished, this woman began resenting God. She even tried to overdose on aspirin because of it. For the next twenty years, she was angry and wanted to run from God. She began drinking and started making the wrong friends. After high school she started college, but she could never seem to find a purpose. Later she became pregnant while in an abusive dating relationship, so she dropped out of college. Knowing that abortion was not an option, she began life as a single parent. And without a college degree, she was only able to work for a few dollars an hour to support herself and her child.

By now she completely entertained thought after thought that she was nothing more than worthless. All this was because she believed thoughts—about God and herself—that the enemy had planted in her mind. Thank God, someone invited her to an on-fire church, and she made the decision to stay, saying, "I stayed because I felt the power of God there." As a result, she later went back and finished her college education so that she could get a good-paying job.

Today she is serving God wholeheartedly and dismissing all previous thoughts of self-rejection and insecurity. When she decided to answer those beliefs and thoughts in her mind, God delivered her mightily. We have to answer those enemies of the mind that are telling us that we will never rise up from the dust and do anything great for God.

Hey, Fig Tree, It's Time to Die

Remember when Jesus encountered the fruitless fig tree on the road the day after He rode into Jerusalem? Hoping for some fruit, He didn't find any on that tree. I don't believe Jesus cursed the tree only to teach His disciples a good faith lesson, even though that was important. I believe He also was warring His own warfare. I think He cursed it because the "lack of fruit" on the tree was a mocking voice in Jesus's soul. Looking at that tree without fruit on it was putting thoughts into His mind. Think carefully about this: what reason would Jesus have for cursing a fruitless tree when it wasn't even its fruit-bearing season (Mark 11:13–14)? That would be like getting angry at an apple tree for not producing apples in the winter. That doesn't make sense. We know Jesus wouldn't curse that tree because of some momentary irritation like that. It makes much more sense to see that the devil tried to use that fruitless tree as a symbol. It was telling Jesus that His ministry, especially back there in Jerusalem the day before, wasn't being truly fruitful or effective.

Think about what had just taken place. Jesus had just left Jerusalem where the people had thrown palm leaves before Him and worshiped Him. Yet immediately following that incredible praise and worship service, He saw people compromising in the temple and selling doves

(Matt. 21:9–15). Then while He was in the temple He healed the lame, and, once again, the Pharisees became furious with Him.

I think Jesus was experiencing an attack on His soul concerning the level of fruitfulness in His ministry. I know this is so because the same thing happens to many pastors. We have powerful services and people are healed and set free, while at the same time people are sinning and compromising in the church. In addition, someone around town gets mad that people got delivered. It can tell you, a good minister who is trying to effectively change lives in your region, that your efforts aren't working. That is why many pastors get discouraged and quit. I can see the devil trying that here with Jesus, but Jesus didn't give in to those mental thoughts. Instead, He cursed the tree as an act of retaliation. Then He used it to teach His disciples how to ward off their own obstacles (Mark 11:22–24).

It is sure a good thing Jesus didn't entertain a thought like that. Yet sometimes when your mind is bombarded, you think it's just you, or that it is the way things are going to turn out. Satan can use objects, people, and events to plant lies in your mind about yourself and your future.

Often you may not realize there is a tree that has grown along your path trying to mock you in your own mind. It doesn't matter how or why your tree grew. It may have grown because of your past or the trauma of abuse and addiction. It may be a tree that grew because of your own fears and insecurities. It could have been planted at random by the devil. Regardless of how it came, today it is trying to tell you that you are not going to win or have any fruit to show for your efforts.

Jesus had to resist that thought just as we do. How did He do it? *He answered the tree!* Mark 11:14 says, "And Jesus answered and said unto it, No man eat fruit of thee hereafter for ever." Yes, Jesus addressed the very thing that was trying to mock Him. Instead of allowing Himself to receive a mental assault that He wasn't bearing enough fruit, He reminded the tree trying to grow up in His mind that its days were numbered: "Yeah, ole fig tree, it's time to die!"

The next day He walked by the same tree (v. 20), and it was dead. That is when He taught His disciples how to do the same thing with mountains that try to enter their lives (vv. 22–24).

You must answer the enemies that come against your mind and tell them they have to leave your soul. Stop allowing the devil to have possession of your will, your intellect, your emotions, your imagination, and your memory. When those constant evil memories try to invade your thoughts, answer them with the Word of God. When your will tells you it doesn't feel like having prayer today, *answer it*. Yes, say it out loud where your own physical ears can hear you. The way to interrupt evil thoughts is with words spoken aloud. When your emotions are screaming and you want to burst out in anger or cry uncontrollably, you can answer it by saying something godly instead. Your imagination will stop running wild when you begin to take authority over it and then fill your mind with other godly things.

Regardless of how the attack comes at your mind, the devil is always plotting how to use your soul against you. Cast him out in the name of Jesus, and tell your mind to be free. God wants your soul realm to be a blessing in your life, not a burden! After all, the Lord gave it to you as a tool to serve Him.

Images in the Dragon Well

God used Nehemiah so powerfully as one of the people who rebuilt Israel's heritage after they came out of their Babylonian captivity. Just as we rise up from our own captivities, Nehemiah also had to answer the enemies who wanted to play on his mind. As soon as he rose up to rebuild the wall of Jerusalem, he was about to encounter many enemies who wanted to tamper with his confidence. But the famous Sanballat and Tobiah rose up first, and, as Nehemiah 2:10 says, "...it grieved them exceedingly...."

Now there is something called anger, but then there's *wrath*. These two weren't just mad; they were mad enough to commit murder. They didn't want the wall rebuilt because it meant they would lose their own positions of control. They are a perfect picture of demon activity that comes to tamper with your life the moment you decide to step into a new season with the Lord. Once you decide to rise up from past captivity and rebuild your new purpose, the devil will be upset because he is going to lose some territory of control. He will do everything he can to stop you. Nehemiah had to learn to stand up to the enemies that came to intimidate his mind.

> And I arose in the night, I and some few men with me; neither told I any man what my God had put in my heart to do at Jerusalem: neither was there any beast with me, save the beast that I rode upon. And I went out by night by the gate of the valley, even before the dragon well, and to the dung port, and viewed the walls of Jerusalem, which were broken down, and the gates thereof were consumed with fire.
> —NEHEMIAH 2:12–13

Notice while he was preparing for the task ahead of him, Nehemiah had to pass several gates. I believe they paint a prophetic example here, which is often why the Bible records specifics like these. First he passed the valley gate, which was the gate that led to the valley of Jehoshaphat, often called the valley of dead bodies because that is where the armies of Ammon and Moab all died when they came against Jehoshaphat (2 Chron. 20:1–26).

Could this have been the same gate Jesus walked through on His way to Calvary? No one is certain. Nehemiah passed through this gate because it represented that he would have to conquer enemies that would seem impossible to defeat (as Jehoshaphat did), but they would all be utterly defeated.

Then Nehemiah went by the dragon well. Now, this body of water was very interesting and carries such an important message concerning mental warfare. The dragon well was a winding well. It received its name because it wound around like a dragon or serpent, but some historical accounts say there was an actual image of a dragon built there after the destruction of Jerusalem. Others say people believed serpents and dragons lived there. In either account, something demonic must have been hanging around for it to receive the name "dragon well."

Nehemiah's passing the dragon well represents overcoming an attack on the mind in a realm we cannot see. Winding things speak of confusion and mental torment that prevent a person from knowing which direction he is going. It is like a drunken person who cannot walk a straight line because he is not in his right mind. Mental attacks will keep you from walking a straight line in the direction God wants you to go. Think about it: One day you are all excited about a new job opportunity. Then something hits your mind, and the next day you are hopeless and discouraged and don't know what to pursue in life. That is because mental images and thoughts have tried to wind you off course. They try to paint a picture of utter despair and defeat about your future. Letting them continue will only make the "dragon image" get bigger and bigger. That's when the image becomes more solidified inside of you until nothing anyone says will make you believe differently.

> When God is talking, it is revelation. You don't have to "talk" yourself through it—you just *know* that you *know.*

In Psalm 55:2, David said, "Hear me and answer me. My thoughts trouble me and I am distraught" (NIV). The word *distraught* in this verse means to be in "a stir" and to "be distracted." When your thoughts are being tampered with, you will soon find yourself off course if you don't know how to deal with them. Nehemiah had to overcome images of failure, discouragement, and insecurity if he was going to rebuild what had been torn down. We have to "pop" the air out of those inflated mental pictures, or we will become suffocated by them.

Then, lastly, I should mention that Nehemiah had to pass by the dung port. This obviously represents a commitment to holiness and a willingness to remove all impurity from your life. Doing so is also a very important step to winning the battles of the mind. If you still have compromise and purposely make plans to keep sinning, then your thoughts will never line up either.

Get to the Source

There are some simple ways to recognize and defeat wrong thoughts that I want to give you here. I also want you to see how to respond properly to godly thoughts. Here are three keys that will get you to the source of your thoughts so you can win the soul battle.

Find the source.

First, decide where the thought originated. If it came from God, then it will reflect His character and the principles of the Bible. It will have a right tone to it. That doesn't mean it will always make you feel instantly happy, because God can speak to correct you. But when He speaks, it will be different. God's voice will speak to your spirit; then you process what He says in your mind.

What I mean by that is this: When God is talking, it affects you like a light bulb. It is revelation that you didn't have to work up in your mind. When God speaks to the spirit of a man, He imparts. It is almost as if you knew it all along! You don't have to talk yourself through it—you just *know* that you *know*. Then your thoughts begin to process and support what the Lord reveals.

On the other hand, when the devil has something to say, somewhere the character of God and principles of the Bible will be compromised.

Usually it feels like you had the wind knocked out of your sails. It is like being punched in the stomach or puffed up in selfishness and pride. Then you "work it up" and "stew" over it. The thoughts keep driving at you as if to say, "Oh, and another thing!" You never feel peaceful or resolved while thinking about it, nor can you find the solution. Here is the biggest key: the devil's thoughts will never drive you to prayer or God. They make you want to sin, backslide, quit church and ministry, run from family, be angry, gossip, or just act badly. If the thought comes and you can't worship God while you are thinking it, then question its source! If you can't pray aloud and talk to God about it with confidence, then it probably didn't come from the Lord.

> If you can win the soul battles and answer the thoughts that come to discourage you, then you will be able to weather the trials of life.

Answer the source.

When a thought comes to you, always do something with it. If it came from the devil, answer him with God's Word the way Jesus did when He said, "It is written..." (See Luke 4:1–14.) Jesus didn't let thoughts and mental attacks go unaddressed. You must respond to the devil's mental attacks with a verbal answer. If thoughts keep telling you that your finances will always be a failure, don't just stew over it. Stand up and say, "I reject that thought. My finances will turn around for the better." If you are too embarrassed and don't want anyone around to hear, then go into another room and say it, but never leave those thoughts unaddressed.

Sometimes we don't answer because we don't want to even admit to ourselves that we had such a thought. But if we allow it to go on, it will keep coming at us. We must let the enemy know where we stand on the subject. As I said before, words said aloud will abort your thoughts because your brain has to change what it was previously thinking when your mouth actually says the words. Then, on the other hand, if God is speaking to you, respond to Him in prayer, worship, and joy. God does speak to us, and He wants us to respond back to Him and be receptive to the things He has to say.

Act on the source.

To act on the source means we have to physically *do* something to support what we *say* about the thought. If the thought was evil, then do something righteous in direct opposition to it. For example, if the thought was about financial failure, you can sow an offering. If it was a thought to discourage your healing, go and minister to the sick. If it was about self-hate and rejection, counter it by doing something nice for yourself and by showing love to others. If your thought was one of fear, then step out in faith. Of course, if God spoke something to you, you will want to show by your actions that you trust Him. Whether the thought came from the Lord or from the devil, always act out in righteousness and you will be blessed.

When we learn to successfully win the battle for our souls, we have crossed one of the biggest hurdles to getting victory after our lives have been tampered with. If you can win the soul battles and answer the thoughts that come to discourage you, then you will be able to weather the trials of life. Remind yourself every day that these battles of the mind have no power to control you. The false imagery of imagination, a defiant will, distraught emotions, a prideful intellect, or a broken memory are no match for the anointing of God and the power of Jesus's name. When your soul has been tampered with, God has empowered you to take back the rightful ownership of your soul and to stay in control of your mind. You should thank Him for that!

Seek him that maketh the seven stars and Orion, and turneth the shadow of death into the morning, and maketh the day dark with night: that calleth for the waters of the sea, and poureth them out upon the face of the earth: The LORD is his name.

[AMOS 5:8]

[CHAPTER 5]

THIS CYCLE of
TROUBLE MUST STOP

S O THERE THEY SAT, VICIOUSLY WORKING UP A PLAN, probably in some secret meeting room during some odd hour of the night. This is usually the setting for this type of conspiracy. Everyone who had sided against the rebuilding of Jerusalem's wall was in on it. "Let's see," they said. "We will wait until they aren't looking and catch them off guard and kill them all!" All previous attempts to interrupt the rebuilding process had not been successful, so now they came to a final resort—murder!

Sanballat was there, along with his coconspirator Tobiah. They rounded up the most evil of leadership from the bands of the Ammonites and Arabians, as well as a group from the city of Ashdod who didn't like what the rebuilding of the wall represented. To them it symbolized a new liberty and a new direction for the people of God and a reclaiming of Israel's own unified identity. Israel's freedom from past captivity meant that their captors were going to lose their territorial control. They didn't like the idea that God's people were erecting a wall between them because to them the wall sent an unspoken message of "Keep out!" Now they were willing to slaughter everyone who was working on the wall and trying to rebuild their broken dreams.

As they organized their crime, however, they had no idea that some of the Jews who lived near them had overheard their plans of attack. At least ten times they warned Nehemiah and his work crew that they were living right under the shadow of certain death (Neh. 4:7–12).

Beneath the Death Shade

Yet with a cycle of constant trouble, having to forge through one perilous event after another, Nehemiah was not going to stop this time, even under the threat of death. No matter what, he was going to rebuild God's promise. He was going raise the walls that Nebuchadnezzar had torn down, even when the attacks against him were unrelenting.

If we are going rebuild our dreams and come back from a spirit of captivity in every area, we will have to expect that the enemy does not play fair. He has enjoyed a certain measure of control in various areas of our lives and doesn't want us to reclaim those things, just as Sanballat and Tobiah didn't want to give up their control. So sometimes the devil will try to create a whirlwind of problems to distract you from the task of rebuilding your life and future dreams.

The walls of Jerusalem that Nehemiah had determined to rebuild carry a special prophetic meaning. Walls speak of your defenses. They represent the fact that you have drawn a line and you don't want any intruder to cross it. People put fences around their businesses and homes for one main purpose: to protect their property by keeping others out. Walls are a declaration of territorial lines. They define spaces that are reserved for a specific purpose or that belong to specific groups or individual people. They are there to send a clear, nonverbal message.

Now you can understand why Nehemiah's adversaries were so angry at the rebuilding of the wall. They were getting the message loud and clear. Suddenly they had to come to terms with the fact that the defenses Nebuchadnezzar had destroyed were being put back into place. So they decided to create a shadow of fear—a death threat.

To live in the shadow of death means you are under a constant dark cloud of some impending disaster. I think of it like a Pink Panther cartoon I saw years ago. Pink was going about his business when a little rain cloud appeared right above his head. Then everywhere he went, the little "dark cloud" followed, hanging over him. It was sunny everywhere else, except in the small space above where he was standing. The cloud followed him into buildings, to his house, and even squeezed itself over and under objects just to harass him.

He even tried to stuff the little rain cloud into a garbage can, but to no avail. No matter what Pink tried, it kept raining. But only on him!

This is what the shadow of death is like. The literal meaning of the biblical phrase "shadow of death" means *death shade*. It is a dark cloud of trouble that keeps trying to take you out. Think for a moment: a shade is created by an object that stands to interfere with any source of light. The light is hindered from casting a glow on anything underneath the object. The only way to remove that shade or shadow is to remove the object obstructing the light. Those obstructions are like trials and troubles that want to keep cycling through until we are completely distracted from rebuilding our dreams for God. They tamper with you until you can't stay focused.

> Cycles of trouble are why many people never find themselves making progress toward their deliverance from captivity or toward their God-given purpose in life.

Cycles of trouble are why many people never find themselves making progress toward their deliverance from captivity or toward their God-given purpose in life. They are just trying to keep their heads above water as they deal with all the problems. An example of this is when someone receives ministry during a powerful church service, then immediately gets off course putting out personal fires throughout the following week. Now that life-changing moment at church is no longer on their mind. They are not focusing on walking out the Word of the Lord they received. Instead, day-to-day surviving consumes them: keeping a naughty child in order, cleaning a flooded basement, calling angry creditors to work out payments, and figuring out what to do about their car that was just totaled.

> You can't find a real purpose in life or rise from the captivity of the past because you're too busy dealing with all the troubles of today.

Then just about the time some of those problems get ironed out, here comes another set. Now their job is on the line, a relative is angry and stirring up trouble, and then to put the icing on the cake, they find out that they need surgery. Could it get any worse? Who cares about trying to work on anger or insecurity problems? Forget trying to quit smoking until you can find some smoother waters. And as far as a future of big dreams for God, they say, "I just can't focus on that right now."

These cycles of trouble tamper with many people's lives, the same way they did for Nehemiah. His troubles had one targeted purpose: to throw him off the mission of rebuilding that wall. That is exactly what the devil wants for you too. He wants to keep you beneath a death shade of problems so you can't focus on becoming all God wants for you. You can't find a real purpose in life or rise from the captivity of the past because you're too busy dealing with all the troubles of today.

Deep in your heart you want to rebuild your spiritual walls and draw that line between you and your past "Nebuchadnezzar captivity," but who really has the time? You can almost hear it: "*Hmm*, yes, Lord, it would be nice to be free, once and for all, from the deep wound created by the divorce, but how can that happen when…Oh, just one moment, please, Billy fell and cut his knee, and the wind just blew the trash can all over the street. I'll be right back and, uh, God… I would like a rain check on the wall rebuilding thing, please!"

There Goes the Fridge

I remember when we bought our first house; it was a stretch of faith and determination. It was a little two-bedroom house with only about one thousand square feet that included a lower-level, half basement. It was small but very cute. We were thrilled about it. Our payment was half of our net income. To this day, I don't know how we managed to talk the bank into giving us the loan, but we did. Of course, we moved from an apartment that already came with appliances, so moving into a house meant we would need to purchase some. We didn't have a lot of money to spend, so the appliances we needed would have to be used ones. We needed a refrigerator, a washer and dryer, and then a microwave. Just four things, but it felt like twenty-five.

My husband bought a newspaper, and we started looking for anyone who was selling the appliances we needed. Yes! There it was, an advertisement in the paper for a little appliance business that someone had in their garage. The ad said, "Refurbished and renewed appliances for good prices!" So off we went.

The business had a large selection of refrigerators. One problem, though: they were either too small, too large, or…brown, awful green, or yellow. *Aaaccckkk!* Please, Lord! I could not bear to put them in our new, little house. Then just as we were leaving, it caught our eye. There it stood, a full-sized, basic, white refrigerator-freezer with a brown handle. It was gorgeous! For just over one hundred dollars, we told the seller we'd take it. He told us honestly that it was more than fifteen years old, but he had "fixed it up" and it worked like a charm.

We also found someone who was selling both a washer and a dryer. They weren't a matching set, but that didn't matter. They too were about twenty years old. We even found a microwave! Everything was set, and we moved into our dream house.

Things seemed fine until we woke up one morning to "break-down" day. It was the cycle of problem appliances. First it was the dryer—*kapooey!* Then the washing machine quit. I was rear-ended in a fender bender. The garbage disposal broke, some of our plumbing went haywire, and, of course, right about the time we thought we were working it all out...yes, there went the fridge! I suspected something was wrong when I reached for some ice cubes in the freezer one morning and put my hand in a pool of water. *Uh, huh!* Yep, the motor quit! That glorious white, refurbished, one-hundred-dollar refrigerator was done.

Then to keep the cycle of trouble consistent, the fridge was packed full of groceries from shopping the previous day. Meat, milk, butter, produce, eggs...and the list goes on. A new house and nothing works while the milk sours on the countertop. We were such happy new homeowners. It's funny now, but boy, it wasn't funny when we had to start ripping our expensive groceries out of the "beauty fridge" and stacking them all over the kitchen. Oh, the microwave actually survived the vicious, death-shade attack.

When the first bit of trouble strikes, you usually try to maintain your spiritual cool. You quote some Scripture, pray and agree, and laugh at the devil. Then when trouble number two hits, you start to express a hint of frustration. By the time the landslide begins, you find out what's really inside you. If you're not as spiritual as you thought you were, you will find yourself saying things like, "Why me, God? It's not fair! I gave an offering, and now this happens!" Then you throw yourself around, cry, and complain. All your spirituality, or lack thereof, comes bubbling up to the surface. Your level of strength becomes clear now for all to see.

Proverbs 24:10 says, "If thou faint in the day of adversity, thy strength is small." That means if a cycle of trouble has come your way and "if thou faint," then something must be done to increase your level of strength to handle the battle at hand. Actually, the word *faint* in this verse literally means "to sink." Sinking means you are slowly being swallowed by something. You could be getting swallowed by the circumstances themselves, but most often you are swallowed by your response to them. If you study the word *faint* further, you will find that the sinking has to do with becoming disheartened. It means you develop a "give-up" spirit because you think the problem is too big for you.

Now, I wish I could say we experienced a picture-perfect miracle to fix all those appliance problems, like someone sticking an envelope in our door containing fifteen hundred dollars or something. That didn't happen. We were rescued from our plight by a miracle Sears credit card, and we bought all new stuff. You see, we were still in God's school of the Spirit. We were learning how to answer our enemies and to fight trouble cycles the spiritual way. Of course, since that time, we have seen so many miracles birthed out of our determined faith that our "Sears salvation" is nothing more than a memory to laugh about.

Now you may be saying, "I understand your problem of broken appliances may have been frustrating, but I am in the middle of some serious warfare!"

It is true, some problems hold no humor. They are sobering issues that without God's intervention someone may die, a family might be separated, or the future seriously affected. Perhaps you are in the aftermath of a series of tragedies and need the strength to recover. Be encouraged because God is an expert at remedies.

> Seek him that maketh the seven stars and Orion, and turneth the shadow of death into the morning, and maketh the day dark with night: that calleth for the waters of the

sea, and poureth them out upon the face of the earth: The Lord is his name.

—Amos 5:8

The promise of this verse is that the Lord has the power to turn the shadow of death into the morning. In other words, He can take some opposing "death shade" that is hanging over your life and remove it so that light can come through again. The reason this scripture tells you to seek the Lord who has the power to move stars and control the seas is because the Holy Spirit wants you to see that your situation is not hard for the Lord. When you turn to God about everything, you find impossibility melting before you. If you forget to seek Him when you are in trouble, you find yourself sinking into despair.

Now God would not express the fact that His power is this mighty if He wasn't ever planning to use it to help you. He doesn't dangle it before you like candy and then say, "Oh, I know it's good, but none for you today because I have My divine reasons." All God is looking for is some determination from you to seek Him for the answer and not give up until that answer comes. He is waiting on your unrelenting faith.

That is what gets God's attention! It is like lighting a spiritual dynamite wick and preparing for an explosion. Faith from our hearts will get this explosive power of God working. Hebrews 11:6 says, "But without faith it is impossible to please him: for he that cometh to God must believe that he is, and that he is a rewarder of them that *diligently seek him*" (emphasis added). God is looking for some diligence to say that you will not give up but will stand on the promise of His power to change what you have been facing.

> When you turn to God about everything, you find impossibility melting before you.

You must have faith that God will step in and stop this cycle of trouble from tampering with you. Seek the Lord with faith—not just a faith that somehow He will help you muddle through the trials. No, you must have the kind of faith that says, "Lord, You are going to do the impossible for me right now. I am expecting to be delivered!" Then choose not to give up that attitude until His mighty power manifests for you.

The Man Who Didn't Give Up

I know a man who didn't give up when his cycle of trouble just kept coming at him. Some years ago, his wife suddenly filed for divorce. With his dreams crumbling, this man found himself left alone with a large child support payment, a car payment, and a payment for the house that his wife and the children were living in. While the bills were piling up, his attorney advised him that bankruptcy was his only option. With every possible obstacle being thrown at him again and again, he forged through with determination. He refused to accept bankruptcy as the easy way out.

Then one day his ex-wife moved in with another man, but still she wouldn't let him have the house he had been paying for. When the court finally ordered that he could have sole possession of it in order to sell it, he came home only to discover it had been completely trashed inside! Today his testimony is that even though the onslaught of trouble seemed unbearable at times, he continued tithing, giving offerings, and going to church. He said, "I followed the biblical principles taught by my pastors, and, as of today, I have never declared bankruptcy, my attorney bills are paid up to date, and I even have a savings account equal to more than two months' worth of my salary in it. I couldn't have imagined this outcome after all these seemingly impossible problems."

Even though he didn't see this landslide of painful problems coming, he didn't give up. Instead, he expected God to fight for him and for his destiny. He was determined to stand for righteousness even when the enemy wanted him to give in to failure. He didn't give up.

Don't React...Respond

Nehemiah could have easily reacted fearfully to the conspiracy of Sanballat and Tobiah. In fact, at one point, he knew they were trying to scare him by sending evil letters about him all around the region (Neh. 6:19). Nehemiah decided a long time ago, however, that he was going to rebuild this wall no matter what. He was determined to see his dreams and promises brought out of captivity even though every imaginable enemy wanted to prevent it. When they conspired to murder him, Nehemiah didn't react. Instead, he responded. A response sends a message, while a reaction only runs from one. Nehemiah's response was:

> Therefore I stationed some of the people behind the lowest points of the wall at the exposed places, posting them by families, with their swords, spears and bows. After I looked things over, I stood up and said to the nobles, the officials and the rest of the people, "Don't be afraid of them. Remember the Lord, who is great and awesome, and fight for your brothers, your sons and your daughters, your wives and your homes."
>
> —NEHEMIAH 4:13–14, NIV

OK, so let's pull out some principles from his response that we can use to respond to our own cycle of trouble.

Organize a battle plan.

Nehemiah could have easily thrown in the towel on the wall-building project, especially knowing that people's lives were on the line. When it gets to that point, you are at the ultimate testing point—the point of quitting. When the storm is that severe, you will usually have people encouraging you to quit. If you don't know how to follow a battle plan with the Lord, then you will look at the surroundings and may find yourself in retreat.

How do you find a battle plan? Well, Nehemiah put weapons in the hands of the people. You have spiritual weapons given to you by the Holy Spirit that are listed in Ephesians 6:11–18. But when the heat is on, do you really make sure they are in your hands? Are you checking to make sure that your belt of truth is shined and ready to operate? Is your faith shield up? Is your sword out and ready for action? Is the name of Jesus in your mouth?

Take your weapon and your battle plan and go stand on the wall you are trying to rebuild. Then use them the way Nehemiah's group did. Use those weapons against that cycle of trouble.

Stay on your post.

Most real spiritual warfare battles are not won in a single day, the same way that natural wars take time. If the enemy is very determined, then you will have to be all the more determined.

One of the reasons so many people never progress to breakthrough is because we are "on and off the wall." One day we are "in faith" about our circumstances, and the next day we're crumbling in frustration. Some days we flee from those circumstances and other days we fight; thus we never accomplish the desired result of victory.

If you are going to win a spiritual war, then you are going to have to stay after it every day. Stay on your post, face the fierceness of the enemy, and stay "in faith."

Examine yourself regularly.

This does not mean you constantly condemn yourself, but that you check to make sure you are obeying God and living right. Notice that Nehemiah "looked things over." In other words, he made sure everyone was where they were supposed to be, staying obedient.

Make sure you don't have hidden sin in your life and that you are speaking right. Your words are very powerful weapons in the avenue to victory. Make sure they line up with God. Proverbs 6:2 says, "Thou art snared with the words of thy mouth...." Also make sure you aren't backsliding through complaining—as the children of Israel did when they were in the wilderness with Moses. God loves you and will speak to you about any necessary adjustments you need to make. Receive those adjustments and make any changes that you need to.

Resist fear.

Resisting fear is so important because fear can immobilize us as few other things can. Nehemiah told the people not to be afraid of their enemies. Remember that fear is the opposite of faith and demons use it to keep you from fully following God. Instead of trusting that the Lord will work miracles, in the back of our minds we are bracing ourselves for another tragedy—just in case. We may try hard not to appear like we believe that, but our actions often give us away because we don't talk like victorious people.

Since fear is an evil spirit because it is not given to us by God (2 Tim. 1:7), the best way to deal with it is through a command. You must tell fear to leave you, in Jesus's name! Tell yourself out loud—on a regular basis—that you are not bound to fear and it has no control over you.

Keep the Lord on your mind.

Nehemiah had to remind the people to keep their thoughts on God. It is easy to start looking at everything going on around you until you forget to think on the Lord. Things and situations can consume you if you're not careful.

Have you ever woken up in the morning, had a great time of prayer, and then became so caught up in events of the day that you felt completely disconnected from the Lord by the end of the day? That is what happens when people get focused on their problems; they forget the Lord while they are trying to fix everything. It is not because we mean to do it, but rather we focus on the circumstances and can allow them to consume us. Then we start creating remedies that God didn't ordain.

Fight for your property.

Have you noticed how problem circumstances always want to steal what belongs to you? They want to take your money, family, health, and happiness. Sometimes we are so sad about things that we don't find the stamina to fight. Nehemiah stirred the people to get mad. You too must decide that it is intolerable for your well-being to be ripped out from under you!

I want to address this one even more in detail because we sometimes let the devil take far too much away from us, and we never get it back.

Fight for Your Stuff

A wonderful woman who attends our church sent me a real-life testimony about fighting for what belongs to you. I love this story! As a single woman trying to make ends meet, she was unexpectedly faced with the fact that her house had gone into foreclosure. Not sure what to do, she just kept tithing, giving offerings, and staying in faith.

Supernaturally, the money she needed to make up the back payments came in! When she sent this money to the bank, they rejected her payment and continued with the foreclosure process. So, while in bed that night, she asked, "Lord, what shall I do?"

> Fear is the opposite of faith, and demons use it to keep you from fully following God.

Do you know the only word she heard in her heart? Loudly the Lord told her, *"Fight!"*

Rather than give in to fear and self-pity, she jumped out of bed and started praying in the Spirit! She took authority over the devil and said, "I claim ownership of this home and I dedicate it to You, Lord!" She came to church the next Sunday, and my husband preached about

> There is no telling what miracles could take place if we would just fight back in the spirit.

what can happen if you refuse to leave God alone about your situation. She said, "Lord, that's a confirmation, and I will not give up!"

Later that week, she came to a women's Bible study that I teach during the week. Unaware of what was happening with her, I prophesied to her that God was going to supernaturally pay for some things. She resubmitted her application to cease the foreclosure, and God intervened with a miracle. She kept her house, praise God! She said, "That situation reminded me that I need to fight further and believe that my entire house is debt free." Do you know what? I have no doubt that with a fighting spirit like that, she will get what she wants.

There is no telling what miracles could take place if we would just fight back in the spirit. Nehemiah's group decided that it was intolerable to let the work on the wall be stopped because of a distraction. So many trials and problems are conceived by the devil, but they are nothing more than distractions. These distractions are to keep you from rebuilding your life again so that you can get beyond stalemate Christianity. When these things try to keep you from your destiny, you have to decide that it is intolerable. God wants to transform you into someone significant in the kingdom. You must not be thrown from that purpose.

The Art of Warfare Building

Nehemiah's people had to become warring builders. They couldn't choose one or the other as many Christians want to do. They had to fight and build at the same time. In Nehemiah 4:15–18, the people had to build holding a hammer in one hand and then hold a weapon while they put the hammer on the nail. There is a real art to that. If you have ever tried to drive a nail into a piece of wood, you will know that is true.

Can you imagine trying to hold a hammer and sword at the same time and actually get something accomplished on either end? I can't imagine it. I try to hang a picture, and then while I hold the little nail and put the hammer to it, the nail drops from my hand and lands behind the couch or somewhere. Then I have to move furniture to get it. That is so irritating! I can't even imagine trying to do it and wield a weapon too.

Often when it comes to spiritual things, we have to drop our building process of rising up from a life of captivity in order to handle the present warfare. That is not God's best. I believe there is an art to building *while* you war. If Nehemiah's people could do it, then so can we! We can learn the art of warfare, building from the example of David and Solomon:

> Thou knowest how that David my father could not build an house unto the name of the LORD his God for the wars which were about him on every side, until the LORD put them under the soles of his feet. But now the LORD my God hath given me rest on every side, so that there is neither adversary nor evil occurrent. And, behold, I purpose to build an house unto the name of the LORD my God....
> —1 KINGS 5:3–5

We see that David could not build the house of the Lord because he was so busy fighting battles. Even though it was in his heart (1 Chron. 22:7), he could not pull it off. David was too busy fighting off his adversaries and troubles.

Does this mean that when problems face us we can't build our destiny for God effectively? No. I believe we can step into a "but now" experience with God. Notice that is what Solomon said: "*But now the LORD my God hath given me rest on every side...*" (1 Kings 5:4, emphasis added). In other words, there may be wars happening everywhere, but then there is a *moment* when everything changes. You cross over into a "but now" place of supernatural peace where God can anoint you to build even while the enemy is raging. You suddenly take on a restful spirit in the midst of trouble.

Solomon's name literally means *peace*. The Spirit of God in you wants to bring you from the mind of warfare into the mind of peace. It doesn't matter what happens around you; all you know is that your God of peace is settling the situation. The power and anointing of God can surround you in such a way that you become unaffected by the enemy roaring at you. Isn't that what Psalm 91 is all about?

Psalm 91:4 says, "He shall cover thee...." God will cover you to protect you from the enemies circling around you. According to Psalm 91, His covering is the reason you don't have to be fearful of terror, pestilence, and destruction. Yes, you can have trials to deal with, *but now* God is covering you so you can get busy building a life that is a mighty testimony to His name. When you allow God to teach you how to become a warfare builder, some cycles of trouble will lose their ability to hold you back.

> The power and anointing of God can surround you in such a way that you become unaffected by the enemy roaring at you.

Begin stepping into warfare building by asking God for His Spirit of peace to rest on you. We have to have faith that the Lord will place a covering of peace on us that calms every storm. It brings the trial to the place where it no longer has a choke hold on us. This is so important because we don't want to become people who attract new trouble by being rattled all the time. Instead, we want to attract the blessings that a lifestyle of peace produces.

Is God Fighting for You?

I need to know today that God is fighting on my behalf. Of course, God loves to defend and care for His children. But we find some important keys in Scripture that will cause God to actively, and with a special kind of jealousy, take up our case against the enemy. God fights for us because we get in agreement with Him and position ourselves for His defense.

Nehemiah's company of warriors not only fought for their destiny, but they also positioned themselves to receive the anointing and power of God to overcome their cycle of trouble. Nehemiah 4:19–20 (NIV) says, "Then I said to the nobles, the officials and the rest of the people, 'The work is extensive and spread out, and we are widely separated from each other along the wall. Wherever you hear the sound of the trumpet, join us there. Our God will fight for us!'"

First of all, they were battling on a very extensive project. Some of the things we have to rebuild in our lives are extensive. For some people, their past Nebuchadnezzar captivity has a deep stronghold. These people in Nehemiah's day had to realize that they could not do the job alone. They were going to need each other. One way the enemy keeps us from rebuilding is through isolation. Either we think we don't need anyone because we are capable of standing strong without help, or we don't think anyone really cares. No matter what you are dealing with, if you have been tampered with in life, you need other Christians to help strengthen you.

After a very busy week in ministry, I don't always feel like attending our church's midweek evening prayer service. Sometimes I just want to go to bed early. Do you know what I am talking about? Normally you love to pray, go to church, and be with other believers, but there are times when you are too overwhelmed and tired. Every time I have ever felt that way, I end up going to the church service, and the moment the music starts and the believers start to pray and worship God, I am refreshed.

Why? Because there is something about rubbing arms with other believers and just being in the same room with them every week that makes all the difference in your warfare—no matter how tired you were when you arrived. We need each other, even if it is for us to just see someone kneeling before the Lord across the room or lifting their hands in praise. The body of Christ will strengthen your warfare even if you don't agree all the time—maybe because someone else's style of worship is different from yours. The key is, we are there to build each other up.

> If we want God to fight for us, it begins by staying in harmony with God's people.

When the early apostles were in the battle of great persecution, they immediately ran to their friends in the Lord. Acts 4:23 says, "And being let go, they went to their own company, and reported all that the chief priests and elders had said unto them." In other words, they couldn't wait to share their trials, testimonies, and experiences in prayer and worship with their friends.

If we want God to fight for us, it begins by staying in harmony with God's people. When the Bible records the phrase, "God shall fight for us," it usually appears in reference to an entire group of people, as it did in Nehemiah. God never defended loners who couldn't find a way to get along with anyone. Some examples of loners are Lucifer, Cain, and Esau.

Now look again at Nehemiah 4:19. The people realized that, because the work was so large, there would be times they would have to be separated from each other on the wall. They knew this type of separation meant they were vulnerable to attack. We are vulnerable to attack when we separate ourselves too much of the time from the body of Christ. Nehemiah had a remedy in verse 20. He basically told the people, "I know we have a huge work to complete that may mean it takes us all in different directions at times. But when I call for us to come together, get over here right away!" (vv. 19–20, paraphrased).

There might be times that rebuilding the walls of your life will keep you busy, but when the church door is open and the call is there for you to get with other Christians, then don't take it lightly. You need them because the enemy is lurking to take you out if you are always alone.

God takes up our case when we stay in unity and fellowship with the people of His kingdom. When God fought for Jehoshaphat against the Ammonites in 2 Chronicles 20, we find that first, the people gathered together (v. 4); then the Lord fought for them (v. 17). It was the same way for Moses when the Israelites stood before the Red Sea. While the children of Israel were gathered together, the Lord took up their case and the sea parted (Exod. 14:14–16). In Revelation 19:14–17, Jesus comes back with the armies of His people alongside Him to wage war on the devil.

Of course, the Lord will help you even when you are alone, but there is something special about the warfare He fights for His people as a whole. Remember, Jesus loves you, but He also loves His corporate church when they group together. He will fight for you privately, but God's mightiest warfare stands in the midst of His gathered people. You can know with assurance that God is fighting for you when you keep yourself in close harmony with the heavenly family. It happens because Psalm 82:1 says, "God standeth in the congregation of the mighty...." There is safety around the people of God. That is where God will fight some of the most defiant enemies.

From Trying to Triumph

Well, you've heard people say, "Try and then try again." It is an important principle to learn in overcoming obstacles. If you trip and fall in the parking lot, then the automatic response is usually to jump right back up before anyone sees you in a heap on the pavement.

The same is true in every area of life. If you find yourself struggling through repeated attempts at defeating difficulties, then the only thing to do is to get up and try again. It is so simple but worth repeating Ephesians 6:13 here because when trouble tries to tamper with us, we often forget to do what this verse says: "Wherefore take unto you the whole armour of God, that ye may be able to withstand in the evil day, and having done all, to stand." It says having *done all*, to stand. That means you do everything possible, everything God has made available to see you through. Then you keep doing it again and again.

> The Lord will fight for you privately, but God's mightiest warfare stands in the midst of His gathered people.

I have talked with people who have been through a trial and will often say, "But I thought I did everything I knew. I am just trying so hard." Well, again, it's good to keep trying, and that's an important start. But there is something more than trying. God wants us to get past just trying and get into winning! Even though you have been "try-ing," somewhere a moment of "tri-umph" needs to appear. You have heard people talk about taking on a winning attitude. I believe one of the main reasons some people seem to attract problems is because they only have a "trying" attitude. Their attempts at winning are laced with self-pity, so they never get through their current cycle of problems and keep getting hit with new ones. Some people even use their multitude of problems as a way to get constant attention; thus they never get free.

Look at what happened to the apostle Paul when he encountered a cycle of trouble. First Thessalonians 2:18 says, "Wherefore we would have come unto you, even I Paul, once and again; but Satan hindered us." The New Living Translation interprets the word *hindered* there as meaning "to be prevented." In other words, the devil stirred up enough problems to keep Paul from reaching his intended destination.

The New Life Version of this scripture says, "We wanted to come to you. I, Paul, have tried to come to you more than once but Satan kept us from coming." Paul was definitely making multiple attempts. He was trying, but nothing was working. Instead of *just trying,* however, he did something. He took his attitude from trying into winning.

Look a few verses down at 1 Thessalonians 3:10–11. Paul is writing to the same group of people and says, "…night and day praying exceedingly that we might see your face, and might perfect that which is lacking in your faith? Now God Himself and our Father, and our Lord Jesus Christ, direct our way unto you." When he kept encountering trouble, what did he do? He started with extreme amounts of intense prayer. Now I am talking *intense* prayer, not just any kind of prayer. There are nice, quiet, reserved prayers, but then there are prayers that come from the bottom of your toes! You birth them out of your heart. This is the kind of prayer Jesus experienced in the Garden of Gethsemane when He prayed so intensely that He began to sweat blood (Luke 22:44).

Paul finally resorted to that level of prayer because the cycle of trouble hindering him was so vicious. I believe Paul was calling on the anointing of God to step in and interrupt the devil's onslaught. If you are in that kind of trouble, you need an anointing from the Lord to empower you.

Then Paul prayed something else that ministers so powerfully to me. He said, "May the Lord '…direct our way unto you' (1 Thess. 3:11)." Another translation says, "Now may our God and Father himself and our Lord Jesus clear the way for us to come to you" (NIV). He practically called on the entire Trinity of God here. I love the way he said it. In a rough paraphrase he is saying, "Yeah, the Father Himself is going to step in!" He sounds like he has had enough. The key here is that Paul was praying a prayer that had the power to remove obstacles standing between himself and his destination. There was some trouble that kept him from getting there again and again. But now enough of just trying. His bold prayer was now aimed at winning!

Remove the Death Shade

Nehemiah, the great wall-building hero, prayed during his cycle of trouble, and he did it when he was really tempted to be afraid. Realize that from the moment Sanballat and Tobiah had conspired to kill him, he was living under a constant death threat. Everywhere he went he had to watch his back. I mean, the people working with him couldn't even change their clothes every day (Neh. 4:23). It was that bad.

I am amazed they kept the project going. Many of us would have aborted the mission long before that time. We would have had a church split, the pastor might have resigned, and the congregation would be in an uproar!

Nehemiah's boldness and commitment to the rebuilding project was so strong, he would not become distracted by the death threat even as fierce as it was becoming. Once, his enemies even tried to trick him into a meeting with them so they could get him in their grip. As always, Nehemiah was onto their tactics. But I get tickled when I read his response to their mischievous invitation: "I sent messengers unto them, saying, I am doing a great work, so that I cannot come down: why should the work cease, whilst I leave it, and come down to you?" (Neh. 6:3). He was not going to let threats, death shades, tricks, or trouble distract him from rebuilding.

What might happen if we reacted that way as we come back from our own personal captive history? Of course, by the time he said these words to his adversary, he had nearly completed his project. His enemies were running out of options and time. You know? Nehemiah was actually winning!

Alas, with one final attempt, his enemies tried to make him afraid.

In a last-ditch effort, the enemy threatened him by saying, "Their hands will get too weak for the work, and it will not be completed" (Neh. 6:9, NIV). Doesn't that sound familiar? Right when you think you cannot go on wielding the sword of the Spirit, the devil jumps on you and says that very thing: "You'll never make it. Don't you feel tired? Go ahead and give up now before you hurt yourself."

But we need to learn some things from Nehemiah. He prayed in a counterattack that brought the construction project into its final completion. One prayer finally broke the shadow of death that had been following him through the entire project. When the enemy told him his hands would be too weak to finish, he prayed, "O God, strengthen my hands." He counterattacked in prayer and asked God to give him exactly what his enemy told him he would never be able to enjoy!

It Shall Not Rise a Second Time

My husband and I know a dear couple in the ministry who determined not to be beaten by a cycle of trouble. It seemed for a time like circumstances of every sort were attempting to take them out. During that season they battled income losses, cancer surgery, foot surgery, throat surgery, and arm surgery—among other things. One onslaught after another was coming their way, making it hard to build the ministry God gave them.

They had received a word from the Lord by a minister who told them, "Your latter years of ministry will be greater than your former ones." They believed that word, but everything seemed to go the opposite way. Of course, they had to stand against discouragement and continually feeling like they were doing something very wrong—that is what your mind wants to tell you. They decided together, however, that they could not accept that lie and directed their frustration and anger toward the cycle of trouble tampering with their lives.

When the wife decided that she was not going to go down, the

Lord spoke in her heart to read Nahum 1:9, which says, "Affliction shall not rise up the second time." That was it! Her cycle of trouble had to cease because she was not going to tolerate another repeat.

> You are not just a conqueror; you are even better than one!

Determine that you will not let the cycles of trouble arise even one more time. It cannot be allowed to tamper freely with your destiny in God. Tell yourself today that it cannot rise a second time. Of course, the devil will always whisper into your ear in order to make you believe you will be overcome. Don't accept it!

The way to stop the cycle of trouble is take the attitude of Nehemiah and decide that every enemy will be defeated and will not rise against you anymore. Know today that the enemy cannot beat you unless you expect him to do so. Remember Romans 8:37 says, "Nay, in all these things we are more than conquerors through him that loved us." You are not just a conqueror; you are even better than one!

You don't have to put up with a constant cycle of trouble. Yes, you will finish rebuilding that wall and God will get all the glory in the end. Nothing will remain except an incredible testimony about what God can do, if you rise to the challenge and command this cycle of trouble to stop.

And it shall come to pass, that like as I have watched over them, to pluck up, and to break down, and to throw down, and to destroy, and to afflict; so will I watch over them, to build, and to plant, saith the LORD.

[JEREMIAH 31:28]

[CHAPTER 6]

The EYE of GOD
IS UPON YOU

O NLY NINETEEN AND LIVING ALONE IN NEW YORK CITY, Sandy was miserable. She hated herself, she was anorexic, and she was entertaining thoughts of suicide. One night, after having not eaten properly for weeks, she decided to go dancing with a few friends. Sandy was determined in her mind to get completely intoxicated in order to forget her troubles for a brief time.

While she was there drinking with her friends, Sandy ran into an old boyfriend who humiliated her in front of the group. Already beaten down inside and now drunk, Sandy ran from the nightclub into the middle of the highway. Determined to die, she wanted to be hit and killed by a car. This was it. She had no intention now of turning back, and, to her knowledge, her friends did not follow her out of the club.

Then she saw the headlights coming toward her. She held her ground as the car got closer. As if in slow motion, Sandy sat waiting to be killed by the oncoming car. It approached close enough for her to see the license plate. Obviously, the driver did not see her sitting there. What happened in the next few moments she did not expect.

Suddenly a man, so she thought, lifted her off the ground and set her neatly on the side of the road just as the car passed. Then just as quickly as it happened, the male figure that grabbed her away from the oncoming car disappeared from view. The driver must not have seen the event because the car never even slowed down. "How strange!" she thought. "I should be dead now. Who grabbed me?" All she could remember was that the "man" who rescued her was huge.

> Even when you don't think He is looking, the eye of God is on you.

Just in time, her friends came outside and saw her being placed on the side of the highway. But no one knew who rescued her.

She went home that night still somewhat devastated that she didn't die but in awe of what happened. Was it a passerby who helped her? Was it one of her friends, or could it be…an angel…or God?

The event caused Sandy to shake uncontrollably for days. Deep inside, she knew. Yes, she knew it had been supernatural. It had to be God who stepped in. Who else could it be? God had been watching her. He saw her pain, and He saw her in the nightclub. God even knew all along that she had wanted to die.

Sandy just had to ask herself: "Why, Lord? Why would You step in and help me? Why did You even care, God? I am nothing." Sandy soon discovered that God had helped her with a miracle because, even when you don't think He is looking, the eye of God is on you.

> Your eyes saw my unformed substance, and in Your book all the days [of my life] were written before ever they took shape, when as yet there was none of them. How precious and weighty also are Your thoughts to me, O God! How vast is the sum of them! If I could count them, they would be more in number than the sand. When I awoke, [could I count to the end] I would still be with You.
> —PSALM 139:16–18, AMP

The extent of how much God is watching you cannot even be counted! You may not feel worth it, but nevertheless, His eye is on you.

It takes a revelation to understand it. It requires an understanding that not every person or even every Christian has received. It is knowing that God is watching you. He watches your every move.

This is often something we accept and verbalize only in theory, but few know how to operate their lives through this powerful truth. Yes, we say things like, "He's got the whole world in His hands" or "He carries me." Do we really know, however, what it means to say, "God is watching us"?

God said to me one day, "Nothing goes unseen by My almighty eye!"

The normal response to a statement like that is, "Well, yes, Lord, I know You see everything." Yet I paused to think, why would God want to say that to me? What did He want me to know? Was I sinning or disappointing Him? No, it was something else. God wanted me to know that when He looks at me during every millisecond of time, something is there waiting to be received. Something can happen at any moment.

When God looks closely at you, inside and out, the unexpected will happen. Once you know the depth of it, not only will you receive the unexpected, but you will also then step into the realm of the unusual. Everything changes when you realize that the eye of God is on you.

The Work Cannot Be Stopped

OK, let's go back to Israel and their long season of Babylonian captivity. In Ezra 1, when Cyrus told them that they could begin rebuilding the temple, they were excited for the task at hand. Something was changing! A new season was dawning on them. Yet even with the king's blessing, they were not prepared for the opposition they were about to face. Just like in the Book of Nehemiah when Nehemiah's enemies didn't want the wall of Jerusalem rebuilt, the enemies of Israel didn't want the temple of Jerusalem rebuilt either.

Remember, when you want to do God's will, someone always has to get stirred up. The heat of resistance was so bad that they had to stop the building of the temple until Darius became king (Ezra 4:5, 23–24). Under his reign, something took place that caused the work on the temple to get started again with fresh vigor. We need this same power to rest on us so that we can build our destiny with the same unrelenting power, the kind of power that blows over the obstacles constantly trying to make us fail. That is why I encourage you not to spend hours asking God why something didn't work out or go the way you had hoped.

You are not alone! All through the Bible, people who served the Lord and did the work of God were attacked vehemently for their efforts. There are too many examples to even list. What we need to focus on is stepping into the miraculous power of God in order to complete the destiny He has for our lives.

In Ezra 5, there were two major factors that caused the building of the temple to resume. I believe they both represent the supernatural ingredients that God wants to give us in order to build our lives as temples of the Holy Spirit. We need an anointing to accomplish that so that the work cannot be stopped. When we try to live right and serve God in our *own* power, we become frustrated by resistance just as the people in Ezra did. This is where many people give up their course and become content staying in some sort of "Babylon."

For Israel's rebuilding of the temple, however, there came a time when God intervened in a supernatural way. That moment changed everything. This is also what *we* need, a moment of intervention.

According to Ezra 3, they were only able to lay the foundation of the temple before the work was stopped by their enemies. Does that sound familiar? We step out to serve God, begin resurrecting our lives from the dust of the past, and the enemy comes to interfere. Tests, trials, and temptations will always try to stop our building process.

So often it seems that many Christians get a good start on some things, and then, after a trial or two, they find themselves falling backward. For example, about the time you start to study the Bible concerning healing and deliverance, the devil will attack you directly in those areas. You get a fresh revelation about tithes and offerings, and your finances take a hit. You just get the foundation laid, and then your adversary shows up. Mark 4:15 says, "And these are they by the way side, where the word is sown; but when they have heard, Satan cometh immediately, and taketh away the word that was sown in their hearts."

Yep! As soon as God gives you a revelation, as soon as that Bible verse comes alive to you, or as soon as that fresh word from the Lord is sown in your heart, here comes the resistance. Just as the foundation is laid, the enemy attempts to pull out all the stops to keep the walls from going up.

Ingredients for Supernatural "Temple Building"

It happened exactly that way for Israel. Ezra 4:23 says the enemies of God's people "made them to cease by force and power." They had excitedly begun the work with all their might, but the work was hindered until God stepped in. He stepped in with two necessary ingredients that we also need to build our "temple" of the Lord. I believe together these ingredients create God's supernatural recipe for us to successfully build lives that are free from bondage.

INGREDIENT 1: *God brought prophetic anointing.*

> At that time the prophets Haggai and Zechariah son of Iddo prophesied to the Jews in Judah and Jerusalem. They prophesied in the name of the God of Israel who was over them. Zerubbabel son of Shealtiel and Jeshua son of Jehozadak responded by starting again to rebuild the

Temple of God in Jerusalem. And the prophets of God
were with them and helped them.

—Ezra 5:1–2, nlt

This means that we constantly need a current word from the Lord.
You cannot continue to do anything successfully without a "now"
word. Notice it was Haggai and Zechariah who prophesied to help
them. I encourage you to read their prophecies in the books of Haggai
and Zechariah. In fact, it was Zechariah who said, "Who art thou,
O great mountain? before Zerubbabel thou shalt become a plain: and
he shall bring forth the headstone thereof with shoutings, crying,
Grace, grace unto it" (Zech. 4:7). What was the prophet doing? He
was prophesying life and power to Zerubbabel's work. The headstone
this prophet was talking about was the final stone, the final piece. He
was saying that the work shall be completed.

We need that kind of prophetic sound that will declare grace
over our lives and our ministries as we build them for God, especially when we are being tampered with by the devil! A prophecy
may come directly to you through someone else; it may be the Word
of the Lord from God's prophets spoken corporately; or it could be
God giving you a simple prophetic revelation privately, whether in
Scripture or just in your heart.
We need prophets and prophecy
to help fuel us with energy. You
can recognize prophetic revelation because it always comes
fresh and it impacts your situation with life and power. Without
the prophetic word, we only fight
with our morals and principles,
but the prophetic word adds current revelation and electricity to our
principles. When the children of Israel had to collect manna every

> You cannot continue
> to do anything
> successfully without
> a "now" word
> from the Lord.

day, it represented the constant need for the fresh word of God in our hearts.

If you want to add the dimension of the prophetic to your building process, begin by listening in your heart. Expect to hear God speak to you in different ways, specifically about your situation and your life. Then when possible, get around solid, good, prophetic churches and people who preach sound doctrine. This will also stir the prophetic in you. Finally, listen to God's recognized and accepted prophets around the body of Christ via media or in person. They will help fuel you with the Word of the Lord to keep your efforts for God fresh and alive.

INGREDIENT 2: *God's eye was upon them.*

> But because their God was watching over them, the leaders of the Jews were not prevented from building until a report was sent to Darius and he returned his decision.
> —EZRA 5:5, NLT

Notice that this scripture doesn't emphasize that God was watching over their work as much as He watched over them. That is because God anoints you for things and makes it personal. God wants to empower you to work for Him, not just empower or bless the work itself. So even though the enemies had previously tried to stop the work through force, this time God watched over His children. We will explore the powerful meaning of this more throughout this chapter. In a nutshell, however, when God watches something, it literally means He is creating a miracle!

Now, when God takes a life that has been tampered with and transforms it into a temple of worship, that alone is nothing short of a miracle. And God will also make the miraculous available throughout the entire building process. That is the way He always did things for people in the Bible, and He will do the same for us right now. Isn't that good? For Israel, God took them from building in their own strength to walking in miracles—from human power to God's power—and the enemy was reduced from using force to a place where none of his schemes could succeed.

Begin to receive a revelation that God is watching you by expecting the unexpected every day. Dwell on miracles more than you dwell on what *might not* go right for you. This is usually where we make our mistakes. We fear or expect that something will go wrong or never get better. Instead, see what can go *right* even when it looks impossible.

> Behold, the eye of the LORD is upon them that fear him, upon them that hope in his mercy; to deliver their soul from death, and to keep them alive in famine.
> —PSALM 33:18–19

That is exactly how you start building confidence that the eye of God is upon you. You expect to be delivered and provided for even when it looks like it cannot happen without a miracle! You see yourself free from addiction even when your flesh presses against you. You visualize God healing you even when there is still pain in your body. You imagine God touching the heart of that person who is away from God even though it seems they will never change. You can also see yourself as the amazing person God destined you to be, even though you feel like a failure. You start to see a miracle in the midst of apparent captivity because you know that the unusual will happen when God is watching you.

The Miracle Ride

My husband and I do everything together. We minister together, we take care of the kids together, we cook and do dishes together, and we often buy groceries together. Once, as I said before, we even attempted gardening together. I guess you could say we are each other's favorite person.

When we first got married, it looked like we would have an eternal destiny for junk cars—together. Now when I say junk, I mean we had some junk. I should have suspected something when he told me that his first car as a teenager was presented to him by his father on the back of a tow truck! My father was military, and we moved often growing up, so I always drove my parents' cars. Neither one of us had ever driven a brand-new car. Our first

> **Expect to be delivered and provided for even when it looks like it cannot happen without a miracle!**

car together was the best one we had ever had. It was already more than six years old when we bought it, and we had to get a loan for it. After that, we drove it for another nine years. Pretty scary, huh? For secondary cars, we would get old ones for free from family and friends. They were always ugly, rusty, and huge.

One of our better second cars was one that we bought for a whopping four hundred dollars, and it was pretty good-looking to us. It was a gray Ford Escort, about twelve years old. To us it was cute because it didn't resemble an aircraft carrier as the other ones did! It had only one problem: we drove around town in a cloud of blue smoke, and it would catch fire under the hood if you let it idle for longer than four or five minutes.

Actually, we didn't know that until one snowy morning my husband went outside to warm it up and came back inside to finish getting ready for work. On a random glance out the window, he saw the flames billowing out from under the hood. We both started running around the living room in shock and terror. Screeching or something, he ran outside and threw piles of snow on the car until the flames were doused. Believe it or not, we continued to drive that car with the knowledge that it could not run idle—ever! Not in the drive-through, not at a stop light, not in a traffic jam, not ever. If you stopped, the rule of thumb was to turn it off and start it again when it was time to go. Regardless, we were determined to keep it because, after all, we had paid out a large investment for this vehicle.

What we didn't realize is that we had begun to form a mind-set that we were always going to drive old cars. We didn't go dream at a new car lot the way some married couples do. We expected to receive old ones. Truthfully, I can't even remember us having a discussion about how "someday when things get better we will have a new car." Not even once!

Junk cars appeared to be our Babylonian captivity forever! God always gave us a nice, clean place to live, but the cars? That was something else. We couldn't seem to break free from them. We had so many options on old cars that we gave them away as offerings. Nevertheless, we took care of them like they were new. We washed them, vacuumed them, and shined them up—the best you can shine rust anyway!

Then one day everything changed. My husband received a phone call from someone whom we knew in a nearby town. The caller said, "Hey, I really need to see you today." Now, we had just come home from a trip and didn't want to be bothered right then because we were tired. Yet the caller persisted.

Finally we agreed, and in a few hours he arrived at our house. We talked for a while in the living room, still not really sure about the purpose of the visit, until we saw him to the door to say good-bye. He asked us to come outside, and then he unexpectedly gave us a key—a car key. It was the key to a brand-new luxury car that was sitting in our driveway. He wanted us to keep it or trade it in on something else we really wanted.

Now, you talk about speechless! I don't think either of us said a word for two whole minutes. We just stood there with our eyes and mouths wide open. Having small children, we did trade in that luxury car for the most beautiful, shiny, new minivan, and to make it special, we bought it right off the showroom floor! It was fully loaded, complete with two stereo systems and a television. And a television in a car was pretty unique that many years ago. We drove away from that car lot in our new miracle ride!

Little did we realize that God was stepping in on our car situation because He had been watching us all those years. When God's eye is upon you, you can expect the unusual. This was the defining moment that turned our car captivity forever. We got rid of the old cars right away, except our best one we kept for a second car. Now, you won't even believe what God did with the only old car we kept, which was now fifteen years old. Just over a year later we loaned it to a friend, who totaled it! But it was the best thing that could have happened to us. Even though the car was snatched from our hands, we got a second beautiful new car that was only a year old.

Our depressing years of car captivity were over in an instant. Why? Because when the eye of God is upon you, everything the devil has tried to keep your mind captive is subject to change just as it changed with the captivity of Israel. When the Israelites couldn't build the temple themselves, God stepped in with a miracle.

Thou God Seest Me

There is a woman in the Bible whose life was tampered with, and she needed God to step in and do something miraculous for her. We don't give a lot of attention to this woman because she seems to play a secondary role in most of our Bible stories. She was someone who became the victim of a marital squabble, caught in circumstances that made her the outcast party. All fingers were pointing at her now, leaving her no other option but to run away. She was an Egyptian named Hagar, the maid of Sarai, who was the famous wife of Abram.

(God later changed their names to Abraham and Sarah.) We find Hagar's story in Genesis 16.

When Sarai couldn't become pregnant by her husband, Abram, she demanded that her husband sleep with Hagar so Sarai could have her child. However, that plan backfired. As soon as Hagar became pregnant, Sarai became angry and jealous and felt her maid was now developing an attitude of disrespect about her successful pregnancy. As a result, Sarai dealt so harshly with Hagar that her pregnant maid ran away. Desperate, Hagar fled into a nearby wilderness to hide. Now she was left alone to carry the emotional burden from a series of events that were not her fault.

But there was someone else watching the entire scenario. Hagar couldn't hide for long because the Lord was watching. She sat there by a fountain of water on the road leading to the wilderness of Shur. I should point out that the Bible often mentions names like this and other similar insignificant details because there is a hidden message behind the natural events. The word *Shur* means "wall." Sometimes when we feel as if we are in a kind of spiritual wilderness, we put up all kinds of emotional walls. We feel hurt and deserted, so we think that becoming closed off to friends, church, family, and circumstances will prevent us from getting hurt again. Whenever you feel like the enemy has come to tamper with your life, it is important you don't put up emotional walls that resist God and other people.

> The wrong kind of walls will cut off God's intervention, while the right, spiritual walls will protect you and cut off the devil's access!

Both men and women do it—each in different ways, but they do. Some walls come in the form of anger toward God or the inability to express love for others. Perhaps the walls compromise our ability to be content in a good church. Many people have unhappy marriages and home lives because of walls built up by past hurts.

God doesn't want you to build walls of hurt. Instead, He wants you to build the kind of walls that keep the devil from tampering with your life, the way Nehemiah did in Jerusalem. God wants you to build walls that define you and set you apart as a holy vessel of the Lord. The wrong kind of walls will cut off God's intervention, while the right, spiritual walls will protect you and cut off the devil's access! There is a vast difference!

The way to know you have built a wrong wall in your heart and mind is when you have to keep referencing one or more painful events from the past to make decisions about the present or future. When you can't seem to express proper love toward someone because you fear being hurt again, you are building wrong walls. If you are unable to develop healthy relationships because of hurtful or improper ones from the past, there are likely some demonic walls that have to be removed from your heart. Hagar was in danger of building the wrong walls in her life walking down the road to Shur, but God was about to intervene.

The best thing she did was sit by a fountain along the way. There, when she didn't know how to fix the situation or even how to face it, God came on the scene. Suddenly Hagar found herself talking with the angel of the Lord, who encouraged her to return to Sarai and assured her that everything would work out. To encourage her, the angel also began to give her a prophetic picture of her future and her pregnancy (Gen. 16:9–12).

For Hagar this was the supernatural intervention she needed. She had probably never before experienced a conversation with a heavenly being. Yet the Lord knew she needed miraculous help during her most desperate time. When she couldn't handle it in her own power, God stepped in with something supernatural. Hagar had to stop heading toward Shur, however, and become settled by the fountain of water.

She had to stop putting up walls and be willing to let God intervene with a miracle.

Had Hagar stayed on the road to Shur, the miracle she experienced might not have happened, and she would have never seen the fountain of blessing right before her. It caused her to stop putting up emotional walls and to start seeing that there was a fountain of blessing instead. As a result, she named the fountain Beer-lahai-roi, which means "to live." This miraculous moment caused her to live again. God longs to give you a supernatural moment so that you can live again too.

Sitting by the fountain positioned Hagar for the most incredible revelation. She came to a conclusion that caused her to be revitalized. Genesis 16:13 says, "And she called the name of the LORD that spake unto her, *Thou God seest me*: for she said, Have I also here looked after him that seeth me?" (emphasis added). While sitting there she saw God step in with supernatural power, causing her to receive a revelation that He had been watching her the whole time! Suddenly she said, "Thou God seest me!"

Notice it was the name she literally gave the Lord. She actually called His name, "the God who sees me." In other words, that was who she knew Him to be in her life. Then she further said, "I have now seen the One who sees me" (v. 13, NIV). She realized when she thought she was painfully alone that God was there all along creating a miracle for her. I believe the "angel" she spoke with was really the Lord Himself.

Once you know that God is watching you, you can begin to expect a miracle; you can expect the unusual to happen. Our trouble is that we take negative circumstances and use them as indicators that God somehow left us. While assuming we are forgotten, we build walls and start to expect something bad to happen again. Never forget that expecting the worst will attract new trouble to you, but expecting the supernatural will open up the miraculous power of God. Realize that your past or present trouble came because there is a real enemy—the devil—who wants to tamper with you. He doesn't care whose life he destroys or whom he makes miserable. He wants to keep you in the grip of hurt and worldly captivity.

There is a way to stop him. We stop him in his tracks when the miraculous power of God intervenes. If we want the Lord to come on the scene with a miracle, we cannot remain on the road toward Shur, building walls of hurt. Instead, we must stop and set ourselves by the fountain of water as Hagar did so we can live again no matter what the past. There we can start to look for the miraculous. It is the defining moment that will cause you to receive the revelation that God is always watching over you, ready to do a miracle. Regardless of the captivity you have previously experienced, you will go from building walls of bondage to building walls of anointing and power.

> In that day shall this song be sung in the land of Judah;
> We have a strong city; salvation will God appoint for walls
> and bulwarks.
>
> —ISAIAH 26:1

The wall Nehemiah rebuilt that we talked about previously represented the walls of salvation or deliverance. These kinds of walls are designed to keep the enemy from harming you in the future. They are spiritual walls of anointing. Now, does that mean Satan won't try to tamper with you? No. It means you have established a way to defend yourself and fight back! Your walls of salvation aren't about hurt and disappointment; now they speak of deliverance and strength.

In whatever area you are rising out of Babylon's captivity, you have to rebuild your temple and your walls. That is what Israel had to do when they rose from Nebuchadnezzar's Babylonian captivity. They had to rebuild the temple (Ezra) and the walls (Nehemiah). Building your temple speaks of changing your lifestyle, character, and habits to reflect godliness. Building your walls speaks of your spiritual power and anointing to stand against the works of the devil. When this verse in Isaiah says God will appoint His delivering power to be your walls, it is saying that God will create a secure defense system for you through His power. Doesn't that sound like a supernatural miracle?

Begin building your walls of salvation today by saying, "God, I know that You see me right now. It doesn't matter what happened before; today I see You watching over me for a miracle." With that revelation, you will see the most incredible miracles of your life!

God, Are You With Me or Not?

Jesus gives us some of the best examples of how to stand confidently and know that God will never leave us. Again, this has to become more than a religious doctrine we admire. It has to be a revelation even when things look bad and we feel like we are all alone.

These testing moments come for everyone. Jesus had to begin His ministry on Earth knowing this because He was going to be tested in it. We talked previously about Luke 4:1–13 when Jesus was tempted by the devil for forty days. One of the tests Jesus passed was knowing that no matter the situation at hand, God was watching over Him. I believe that is one of the main reasons Jesus always walked in the supernatural. His confidence in God's presence while facing the darkest, most impossible situations resulted in miracles. Jesus passed that test in the wilderness so that, in the future, He could withstand against the devil's whispers saying perhaps God had left Him.

Looking again at Luke 4:9–12, we find the devil encouraging Jesus to throw Himself from the highest point of the temple and then expect God to prove His power through a miracle of saving Jesus from death. Jesus responded by saying, "...Thou shalt not tempt the Lord thy God" (v. 12).

Realize that expecting God to do miracles is different from expecting Him to prove His presence through one. Instead, we have to believe in His presence before we see the miracle. People who ask

God to prove that He didn't desert them by showing some super-natural sign are tempting the Lord.

We see this further in Exodus. When the children of Israel tempted the Lord, they were angry both at Moses and God because there was no water. They were in a thirsty wilderness where it didn't even look possible to locate a water source. It was a trial. The Bible says they argued with Moses (Exod. 17:2). What did they argue about? Whether God had deserted them in their wilderness: "...because of the chiding [arguing] of the children of Israel, and because they tempted the LORD, saying, Is the LORD among us, or not?" (v. 7). How did they tempt the Lord? They kept questioning whether the Lord was still with them.

> Instead of asking God to *prove* His presence, start asking Him for a *revelation* of His presence.

Think about it: how many times have we done that? There we are, facing a challenge or trial, and we begin saying things like, "God, are You still there, because I feel all alone right now." Then we sometimes go further saying, "God, if You are with me, why don't You do something? Where are You? If I could just see You with my physical eyes, I would know for sure You are there." You see, that is not expecting a miracle; it is questioning why you aren't seeing one.

That is what the devil wanted Jesus to do. Jesus didn't have to jump from the temple and "see something" to know if God would show up for Him. Jesus knew God was there, no matter what. As a result, miracles followed Him all the time. Jesus didn't need proof of the miraculous. He just expected it to be there when He needed it. His confidence that God's eye was upon Him was not based on what He saw; it was based on what He knew!

Instead of asking God to *prove* His presence, start asking Him for a *revelation* of His presence. In that setting God can impart some amazing things and you will learn to trust His power.

I received a testimony from a man who told me that he had the most supernatural experience one time when he asked the Lord for a revelation of His presence. As a brand-new Christian, he was still very unsure of the reality of Jesus. His life had been filled with torment, gang violence, and fear. He said, "One day, not knowing where to turn, I grabbed a Bible and decided to attend a church." There he gave his heart to the Lord, but his past taught him to expect disappointment, so he feared that God would fail him.

Once, after a particularly bad day, he was feeling down on himself. Crying uncontrollably, all he had the strength to say was, "God, make Yourself real to me." You see, he needed a *solid* revelation of God's presence, the kind that never leaves you. Jesus had to receive that kind of revelation, and this man was about to receive it too. Right after he prayed his most desperate prayer, a hand literally touched him on the shoulder and he heard the Lord say, "I'll be back for you." From that day on he was never the same. He knew that no matter what he faced in the future, the Lord would come again and again and touch him in the middle of his situation. He received a revelation that God was watching him.

Your experience to receive the revelation that God is watching you may come differently than anyone else's. But ask the Lord to give you this firmly in your heart so that you know His presence is always there to intervene in your most impossible situations. Once you settle that, you don't need to ask God to prove Himself through miracles anymore. Instead, you just expect Him to *miraculously* "be back for you" again and again!

It's Time to Pick Up the Pace

When God intervenes in your situation to bring you from captivity into blessing, the miracles may not come the way you expect. In fact, they usually arrive and catch us off guard, as it did with Hagar. Whenever God moves in with the anointing, it comes with a rush.

Remember the Day of Pentecost? The Holy Spirit came as the sound of a "rushing mighty wind" (Acts 2:1–4). And remember when Israel was trying so hard to recover themselves from the dust and ashes that Nebuchadnezzar had left them in? God suddenly caused them to step into high gear. In fact, the work on the temple went from a slow pace to a speedy one. When God's eye began to oversee their work, they were able to produce the most incredible craftsmanship, and in record timing. Their work took on superhuman speed.

Ezra 5:8 says, "...we went into the province of Judea, to the house of the great God, which is builded with great stones, and timber is laid in the walls, and this work goeth fast on, and prospereth in their hands." God really picked up the pace for them. When God's eye is upon you, He will accelerate your rebuilding process. Let's look at some of the hidden principles from this verse to see what we can expect to happen when God picks up the pace.

> God will manifest your greatest miracles through some of the weakest areas of your life.

They built with great stones.

Stones speak of people. First Peter 2:5 says, "Ye also, as lively stones, are built up a spiritual house...." When God is watching over the building of your life, you can expect He will make it great. God doesn't work with useless stones; He uses great ones. So it doesn't matter what your past habits, challenges, or hurts have been. Today God is rebuilding you as a great stone.

You might be quick to ask, "How can God make something great with me?" The answer is: He does it by miraculous means. You can't always explain the supernatural; you just believe it and expect it. You can't always figure out how God suddenly changes the hardest of hearts or instantly delivers someone from fear or depression. He just does it. When the eye of God is upon you, you know He is going to make you a great stone.

They used timber in the walls.

This is so powerful because timber always represents the imperfection of our flesh. When the ark of the covenant was built in the Old Testament, it was wood on the inside and overlaid with gold on the outside. It was a picture of Jesus who was divinely God (gold) and also very human (wood).

When God works on rebuilding a life that was tampered with, He takes imperfect flesh and uses it to operate in His miraculous power. God takes people with flaws and causes them to do miracles! That is why we shouldn't become critical of other Christian brothers and sisters who sometimes seem to offend us. We are all human vessels being used by God to build spiritual walls that will destroy the works of darkness.

When God's eye is on you, He will miraculously use the very flesh you thought to be so unworthy to tear down Satan's strongholds. Do you realize what that means? It means God will manifest your greatest miracles through some of the weakest areas of your life. God builds supernatural walls with wood.

The work went very fast.

Often we want God to change our situations quickly, but most of the time we aren't prepared for quick change. Instead, we are creatures of habit. When you are armed with a fresh, prophetic word and God is watching over you, then get ready for something quick to happen.

That doesn't mean we skip the process of rebuilding. Rather it means the process will force us into sudden changes every day. Sometimes it means we have to change our schedule. It may mean changing where you live or some of your closest friends. It might involve your financial habits, eating habits, and some of the things you say. When God does a quick work, it can turn your life upside down and you must decide if you are prepared for it. For Israel, they began to build very fast. That probably means there was not a lot of time for vacations and coffee breaks. Maybe they had to schedule working around the clock. Maybe it meant they had to increase staff. For us, when God begins to take an area of our lives and pick up the pace of rebuilding, it will mean we must be prepared to adjust to changes. And those changes may not come at a pace we feel comfortable with.

I have found out that God doesn't always move at our level of comfort. Instead, we just have to hang on for the ride! When Jesus suddenly cast the demon out of the madman in Gadara, I'm sure the man and everyone who knew him had to make some changes to accommodate the sudden miracle (Mark 5:1–19). He now had to move back to town, buy clothes, work, and live in a house. Imagine being the landlord asked to rent this notorious person a home. Just a few days before, he was screaming, insane, and cutting himself! His quick miracle catapulted him into a whole new lifestyle. When the miracle comes fast, are you ready?

The work prospered in their hands.

The Bible tells us that when we set ourselves to please God, He will make us prosper. It means we are suddenly able to accomplish what could not be done before. Deuteronomy 28:8 says God will bless all we set our hands to. In other words, He will make it successful.

> God doesn't always move at our level of comfort. Instead, we just have to hang on for the ride!

It doesn't matter if your upbringing was very negative or if your family experienced one bad thing after another. Maybe none of your relatives graduated from college. That does not have to be the case for you. There may not be any money to pay for college, but if your heart's desire is to go to school and you are living for God, then He will make your efforts prosper. Your circumstances up to this very present day could have been very bad, but when God's eye is on you, then everything you touch begins to be blessed. What everyone says you cannot do, you begin to walk into with supernatural ability.

You see, when God's eye is upon you, you must begin to expect the miraculous. The Bible tells us that God watches over us carefully. As His children we are the apple of His eye. (See Psalm 17:8; Zechariah 2:8.) The devil has used all of your past disappointments and captivity as a way to diminish your expectancy for supernatural intervention. Now, instead of having faith for a miracle, you fear you won't receive one because you didn't seem to get one on a previous occasion. Rather than seeing a healing, you brace yourself for a tragedy because of what a past experience taught you. We say that we believe God watches over us, but our actions and words express fear of the unknown or fear of what might not happen.

Don't believe that! When God watches over something, He does miracles and causes things to prosper. He takes a life that was once invaded by the devil and raises it up supernaturally. God doesn't watch over us and then sit there in heaven while we are drowning just to see how long we can hold out. That is what religion has so often led us to believe. The truth is: He watches so He can step in and miraculously intervene in what we cannot do by ourselves! The reason we don't see *more* of His intervention is because we don't *expect it* to appear.

Set Up a Miracle Watch

If God is watching over us, then we have to change what we watch over. That means changing what you see internally. Start watching for the supernatural. I know people who ask things like, "Why don't I seem to hear from God?" Well, there may be any number of reasons why you don't think you are hearing Him, but it begins by expecting to hear Him. If you believe you won't, then you won't. That principle applies to every part of your life. It is absolutely necessary if you are going to rise up again. Watch for miracles instead of watching for trouble.

> And it shall come to pass, that like as I have watched over them, to pluck up, and to break down, and to throw down, and to destroy, and to afflict; so will I watch over them, to build, and to plant, saith the LORD.
>
> —JEREMIAH 31:28

In other words, you can receive this verse to say whatever victories you have won before should be your measuring stick now. As the Lord walked you through impossible situations before, then He will watch over you this time with that same level of intervention. Stop referencing the disappointments and start watching for the unusual blessings. As God watches over you, start watching for Him. Get up in the morning and say, "This is my day for a healing," or "This is the day that so-and-so will get saved."

Begin to see a miracle and talk about it. I like to say it this way: set up a miracle watch! If you don't make the habit of watching for God's miraculous intervention, then even when it comes you won't notice. If you watch for miracles, however, then you will see them manifest. Know that in the same way you miraculously overthrew the devil's work in the past, this time you will do the same miracles—and *more*—because that is what must happen when the eye of the Lord is upon you!

*Come, and let us build up the wall . . . that
we be no more a reproach.*

[NEHEMIAH 2:17]

[CHAPTER 7]

FIND and REBUILD YOUR
GOD-GIVEN PURPOSE

I JUST SAT THERE STARING BLANKLY AT MY PAPER THAT morning. What was I going to write? Everyone else in the class was confidently penning their future career plans—everyone except me, or so it seemed. That was the picture on the morning of career day during my senior year of high school. All the seniors of my Christian school were supposed to be filling out their future college and career plans for the school yearbook and for presentation before graduation. Like most seniors, we were given practice that year filling out college and job applications and learning to write résumés and reports on what we wanted to do after high school. I kept reaffirming to myself that I didn't have any direction.

I hated those days. They felt like being sent to the torture chamber! Today I realize that it is normal for students to not know exactly what they want to do after high school. I was in a small Christian school, however, in a very small Florida town—there were only ten in my graduating class! *Everyone* had a plan for the future.

Back then, some people had a certain mind-set about what young girls should do after high school. College was certainly encouraged, but I had a sense that there were some occupations my conservative Christian school didn't consider as options for women. I needed a purpose in life that I could put on paper at school that everyone would accept.

I was a Spirit-filled Christian then, but I didn't know what to do with myself after graduation. The obvious answer should have been to start college and figure it all out as I went along. That is what most young people do when they don't yet have a career direction. But there was a problem. Deep down I did have a career direction, but I had trouble admitting it to anyone. I knew it was one my teachers and classmates were going to find odd for a young woman. It was not going to fit in with the yearbook that went out to all the families and parents. Even worse was that I didn't know how to get started on it, so how in the world was this little high school senior going to convince anyone else of her dream?

> Without the skill of knowing how to fulfill your purpose and staying on course with it, you will stay in captivity.

The truth is, I wanted to be a preacher.

Imagine...a woman preacher! "Oh! Anything but that!" That is what I would have heard people say. I knew that for the group I was around, it was about as close as you could get to sacrilege. A girl right out of high school pursuing a career in the pulpit? That just wasn't done!

Now, I could have told them that I wanted to be a nice pastor's wife someday. They would have accepted that. But I knew that would only fuel questions I didn't want to answer. They already didn't agree with the church I went to because it was not a conservative denominational church. I went to the charismatic church in a nearby town. Plus, women preachers were much rarer back then, even in some of my church circles. Now, I wouldn't have minded being a pastor's wife, but I wanted to preach too. The problem was, as a girl, I was too embarrassed to admit it. I am ashamed today that because I feared persecution over my dream in life, I wrote on my career sheet that I wanted to grow up and become a secretary. And even though there is *nothing* wrong with being a secretary, it wasn't what I had in my heart to do. Instead, it was what a girl was *expected* to do.

You see, not only was I afraid to admit who I wanted to be, but I didn't even know how to get my purpose in life started. If there is one single thing the devil likes to do with people, it is to keep them feeling lost in their sense of purpose. They wander though life with no clear direction. Then if they do get a direction for their purpose in life, so many people struggle to maintain any tangible results. To add to the problem, life's experiences and previous trials will attempt to further defer your hope.

I wanted to dismiss the idea of being a preacher because I knew people didn't agree with it. I didn't know it then, but the enemy was tampering with my ultimate purpose and my confidence. He was covertly using people, their opinions, and my own lack of knowledge to prevent me from pursuing God's will for me.

Without the skill of knowing how to fulfill your purpose and staying on course with it, you will stay in captivity because something will always come to distract or discourage you. Something will tell you that you didn't have the right upbringing; you are from the wrong social class; your racial heritage is a hindrance; or even your gender is a problem, as was the case for me. You can also become disillusioned by lack of finances, your current location, or the opinions of your family and friends. These things will tamper with you just enough so you never get anything done.

Something Has to Be Done

Nehemiah had tolerated enough of nothing happening. The wall had been burned down and left in that condition for more than one hundred years. No one had even tried to repair it. In Nehemiah's mind, it was not acceptable to leave things this way any longer. Something had to be done once and for all. It didn't matter that certain people were upset at what he was planning to do. He could no longer live with the current circumstances. He took a personal responsibility to change it, and rebuilding the wall burned in his heart.

Someone had to rise up and do something about the condition of Jerusalem. So for three days Nehemiah came to the city to survey what had to be done. He had the idea to do something no one else had attempted, and he even went to the king for permission. With the king's blessing, he started out. Now came the time, however, for surveying the terrain and counting the cost. It was time to get down to business. He was soon to find that this was going to be no small undertaking.

Quietly at night, with only a small handful of people, Nehemiah went to decide how to get started (Neh. 2:9–18). During those three days, there was probably a great deal going on in his mind. "Wow, this is a lot worse than I anticipated," he might have thought. Nehemiah probably had to reflect on himself, his skills, and his leadership ability. Could he pull this off? How long would it take? Was he the man for the job, and did he have the resources to finish it? I am sure his mind's eye could see all the negatives, his own weaknesses, and the sheer magnitude of the job. Then what were his closest friends and neighbors going to say?

So, with all the normal questions and the cards stacked against him, what made him forge through? Nehemiah had to decide that this was his purpose in life. It was not someone else's purpose, but his purpose. It was going to take some sacrifice, but it had to be done. God's city was in ruins, and it had to be rebuilt. He had to make rebuilding the wall his personal project because he decided it was unacceptable for the city to be left in ruins from Babylon's invasion.

In Nehemiah 2:17 he said, "Come, and let us build up the wall of Jerusalem, that we be no more a reproach." If he didn't do something, then their future would end up a disgrace. This is not what God intended. The city was tampered with and needed a new purpose. If he didn't do something, it was obvious that no one else would.

Now we have to ask ourselves some similar questions. Our lives do not have to remain a reproach. It doesn't matter how you were raised, who betrayed you, or what failure has surrounded you. Everyone has a divine purpose in God to rebuild what was once left in dust and ashes. That will require us to count the costs and begin to walk it out.

In this chapter I want to give some principles from Nehemiah and others in the Bible that will help you build and fulfill God's precise and unique purpose for your life. One of the greatest ways to undo how the devil has tampered with you and others is to have a defined sense of purpose for life beyond the normal things like growing up, getting married, finding a job, and buying a house. Of course, your purpose will involve those things, but we are also designed to have a special God-purpose. That is a purpose to change the negative and build something that will give praise and honor to God.

When your purpose and your life have been tampered with, there comes a point where you tell yourself that your current condition is no longer acceptable and something must be done to change things. This could apply to one area of your life or to many. You finally set your eye on the goal and will not make any more excuses for failure. The problem is that many Christians don't define their purpose. And some who know their call in life don't want to walk through the learning process needed to fulfill it.

The Bible paints this picture clearly in the famous verse of Scripture found in Hosea 4:6: "My people are destroyed for lack of knowledge...." This verse can be applied a number of ways, but essentially a lack of knowledge speaks of ignorance in a certain area. Ignorance about your purpose will keep you captive to the world's system—the system of Babylon. Like Nehemiah, we are going to have to define our purpose and then be willing to pay the price so that we can rise up and do something mighty for the Lord.

Live on Purpose

Floundering is the mistake of many Christians who think that God will just cause them to stumble onto success. They live every day through trial and error, hoping to make all the right decisions. Now, I am not saying that you won't ever have to step into things without a clear direction, because often that is what living by faith is all about. What I am saying is that hoping and guessing should not be the main pattern to how you live your life.

Should I buy that house or not? Should I become a nurse or something else? Should I marry that person? Am I called to ministry? The list of back-and-forth guessing continues. Instead, God wants you to live for Him on purpose. This means that, overall, you know exactly where you are headed. It doesn't mean the path along the way won't look cloudy sometimes. No. Instead, you know you are on the right path, so even when things get dark and confusing, you are following God in the right direction.

Not living with a purpose will keep you captive to the wrong things. For example, if you are single and don't have a clear direction about what you want in a future spouse, you may find yourself marrying someone who is not God's best for you. When someone attractive comes along and flatters you, you will convince yourself that they are the right one. As a result, many people are captive to marriages in which they are miserable. Once that area of your life has been tampered with, it is all the harder to get back on course with God.

Of course, that is just one example. If you don't live on purpose, you are susceptible to the devil trespassing into your territory in any number of ways.

Peter became susceptible to attack by the devil when he forgot his purpose. He only made that mistake once, however, and then never again! After Jesus was arrested, Peter was watching the events leading up to the Crucifixion just outside the palace of the high priest (John 18:15–26). If you remember the story, Peter was asked three times if he was one of Jesus's disciples. The fear of circumstances intimidated him into becoming ashamed of who he was, and he denied being one of the Twelve. You see, when the negative circumstances began to stack against him, he caved. It made him question all the things Jesus had taught him about his future. The current situation was starting to tamper with his calling.

For Peter, along with some of the other disciples, they were so thrown off course by the death of Jesus, they even went back to fishing. That was not what they were supposed to be doing! In fact, they completely ignored everything Jesus said to them about His glorious resurrection. Jesus told them plainly that He

> Know you are on the right path, so even when things get dark and confusing, you are following God in the right direction.

would rise from the dead and go ahead of them back into Galilee and then meet up with them there (Mark 14:28; 16:7). Then when Jesus finally met them, they were on the road heading toward Emmaus (Luke 24:13), just about seven miles from Jerusalem. They were nowhere near Galilee and were nearly fifty miles off course! Maybe they would have gotten there eventually, but I think if they were truly expecting Jesus to rise from the dead and head in that direction, they would have had more of a head start.

I am not sure why Jesus went on the road to Emmaus and made a point to find them. It was probably because He knew those guys weren't going to make the Galilee rendezvous, so He decided He had better go after them. Then when Jesus finally drew near to them along the road, they didn't even recognize Him. The Bible says, "Their eyes were held, so that they did not recognize Him" (Luke 24:16, AMP). I don't believe their eyes were held because God intended it. I believe it was their habit of fear, unbelief, and lack of direction that ultimately blinded them.

Then to top it off, they had the audacity to question if Jesus was really the Messiah! It is almost humorous to read as they unknowingly began to relay their ignorance to Jesus Himself: "But we were hoping that it was He Who would redeem and set Israel free. Yes, and besides all this, it is now the third day since these things occurred" (v. 21, AMP). To me a paraphrase of their words would read something like this: "Well, we thought He was the one, but He didn't do what we expected and now He is dead. Plus, He said He would rise in three days and we haven't heard any news. It must not have been true!"

Their babbling finally made Jesus angry, and He told them that they were too quick to fall into unbelief. How embarrassed they must have been. I almost blush for them when I read it, even though we have all done exactly the same thing at times. Remember that when Peter forgot who he was and what he was supposed to be doing, he got off course.

Then after Pentecost, Peter's response to pressure was an entirely different story. This time in Acts 2–3, he was fearless in his preaching when people began to question his Pentecostal experience and the miracle that healed the lame man. He even confronted the listeners about crucifying the Messiah (Acts 4:10). He was suddenly willing to face persecution and any kind of trial to walk out his God-given purpose. Later he boldly began his letters announcing himself to be an apostle of the Lord.

Why the change? Well, not only was Peter filled with the Holy Ghost and power, but also this time he refused to come away from his purpose and what the Lord had commissioned him to do. He defined who he was and stayed on track. Peter lived on purpose.

Your Fourfold Purpose

Fulfilling our God-given purpose first begins with defining it in detail. I want to lay out a basic blueprint in a simple four-part pattern. We will see that Nehemiah followed the basics of this pattern; so did Jesus. We will list the four parts and define them briefly here and then study them for the remainder of the chapter. Your fourfold purpose is:

1. *Destroy your Babylon.* Ask yourself, "What conditions am I tired of living under?" This means you will have to address your weak points, whether they are sin habits, past hurts, or attitude adjustments. Regardless of how that little bit of "Nebuchadnezzar" may have broken in, you have to clean it out instead of getting comfortable with its presence and the lifestyle that comes with it. Whatever your trouble spots are, they will come back to tamper with you again if you ignore them.

2. *Find your post.* Ask yourself, "What do I see myself doing long term?" You will have to find the main area(s) where God wants you focused in life. This involves the large decisions such as your career path, marriage, and church. It means you have to define your talents and determine what God graced you for and what He didn't. Some of the details along the way may change, but how do you want to spend the majority of time before you get to heaven someday? That is where you have to remain steadfast without distraction.

3. *Build your house.* Ask yourself, "What am I drawn to work on every day?" Once you know what God wants you to be doing, then you have to find the resolve to start doing it. This is where you count the cost and survey the territory. You may have to take a look at your finances, think about the next five years, and then start getting into position. You may have to go to school. You will have to make sacrifices and decide

what things you will have to change and what things are not flexible in your plans. Building your house involves your private walk with God, your position in God's kingdom, and your family life.

4. *Restore your heritage.* Ask yourself, "What do I want to leave behind?" It means reclaiming blessings and benefits you or someone else would not have enjoyed otherwise. Restoring your heritage always involves people far beyond yourself, not just materially but also spiritually. What are you and others being deprived of if restoration doesn't occur? You may need to undo some prior generational curses and turn them into generational blessings. It is like restoring an old house. You can't just paint it and make obvious repairs. You have to find the builder's original design and then bring the house back to its original beauty and heritage.

BLUEPRINT STEP #1: Destroy Your Babylon

If Nehemiah was going to rebuild the wall of Jerusalem, he had a few challenges to address. First and foremost, there were a whole lot of people who had become used to the way things were. So then, what was the real problem? Maybe it was best to leave the wall alone. Yes, maybe there were some dangers near the ruins, but aside from that, was it really a problem? People around the territory were used to it by now.

Had the broken wall of Jerusalem existed in our modern day, it would have become one of the wonders of the world and a possible tourist attraction. Maybe it was a tourist attraction then; who knows? There might have been money in it. The important thing was that people were used to how things had progressed, so Nehemiah was going to have some convincing to do in order to rebuild. Little did he know how much the spirit of Nebuchadnezzar's captivity in Babylon was going to plague him throughout the project. Be prepared when you grab hold of your God-given purpose; some people will fight to stay in bondage and want you to stay there right along with them.

You see, we will have to look at our broken walls and defense systems square in the face if we are going to rebuild. Nehemiah began by taking in the reality of the whole thing. After he looked things over, he came back with this report: "Then said I unto them, Ye see the distress that we are in, how Jerusalem lieth waste, and the gates thereof are burned with fire" (Neh. 2:17). He began by addressing what needed to be fixed. This is the first step to tearing down the spirit of Babylon in your life.

If you know you have an anger or jealousy problem, then don't try to act like it is not there. Perhaps laziness and disorganization have plagued your entire life. Pride, depression, addiction, gluttony, fear, unforgiveness, perversions, gossip, deceit, and more all have to be addressed and destroyed. That is called becoming crucified with Christ. In Galatians 2:20, Paul said, "My old self has been crucified with Christ. It is no longer I who live, but Christ lives in me" (NLT).

Whatever it is, address it in your heart. If needed, address and confess it to someone else. This will only help you destroy it. Chances are the people closest to you already know it. There is a long list of little "Babylonian" attitudes that we pick up along life's road, and people around us can often see them.

Remember I told you that I didn't want to tell my high school class that I wanted to be a preacher? That scenario made it hard early on for me to start seeing myself in the ministry. A few years later, before I married, I was in a good church that even believed in women preachers. In fact, the pastor's wife was a minister and a very capti- vating speaker. The people in the church loved her ministry, so there was no problem with women in ministry there. Yet when asked by people what I wanted to do with my life, I still found myself captive to a lack of confidence that women should admit they wanted to pursue full-time ministry. I would avoid the subject and say something like, "Oh, I want to do something ministerial, you know, like teach people."

They would say, "You mean like a missionary or Sunday school teacher?"

My response would be, "Sure, yeah."

> We have to admit our weak areas so they don't rise up and try to hinder our futures.

Then if we're not careful, our attitude on the thing will attract a spirit of defeat to us. As a result, we have a weak area hanging onto our lives. I had to learn back then how to fight that spirit and declare I was called and anointed of God to preach across the world. As a result, I am now fulfilling that ministry call with victory! That is how you crucify the spirit of Babylon—acknowledge it and address it!

I believe one of the largest, most hindering spirits that tries to keep people captive in Babylon is the spirit of rejection. Nearly every human being has dealt with it in some form or another. People feel rejected because of their appearance, culture, religious background, family, race, gender, education, personality, and more. Satan wants to keep you feeling rejected so you won't rise up and do anything substantial because you don't feel worthy or confident.

We have to admit our weak areas so they don't rise up and try to hinder our futures. Now, we shouldn't beat ourselves over the head about them so that we never find a sense of victory. Truthfully, sometimes we have to laugh at ourselves and visualize our weaknesses as easy to overcome. The important thing is to be aware of the "areas of distress" just as Nehemiah was when he rose up to fulfill the purposes of God.

The first way to destroy the captivity of Babylon is by defining the areas in which it has a stronghold over you. Are there personality weaknesses that make you gravitate toward certain sinful behaviors? Are there ways that you treat people because of how you were treated growing up? Decide the important issues, and then you will be positioned to tear them down. For example, the reason some people cannot get free from gossip is because they don't recognize or see that they gossip. They don't think they have a problem with their mouth. They enjoy opening their ears to the latest and juiciest information. That is a Babylon they are not sure they want to do without. We have to decide how badly we want to be free from these areas.

Free From Perversion in Babylon

I received a story from someone who told me how God delivered them from the tormenting spirit of sexual perversion. It is such an incredible testimony about how to remove the captivity of Babylon from your life. It is more than just a deliverance story; it is a story about rebuilding again after a life was tampered with by the devil. I want to share it here because so many people find deliverance in this area embarrassing and fear exposing it. The testimony was from a woman who, before she had become a Christian, had experienced numerous perverse sexual relationships—both heterosexual and homosexual—from the time she was very young. The devil had targeted her for evil.

Growing up, she found herself as a young woman in all sorts of sexual situations, many of which she hated. Because of so much exposure to it, however, she still craved these perversions even though deep inside she wanted to be free. Remember, patterns and habits of darkness can get programmed into your flesh and soul until you only know how to respond to the wrong things. Evil spirits bank on the fact that your flesh will learn a certain pattern through exposure, and they use that mental recording inside to control countless people.

Finally, she met her husband. They fell deeply in love, and eventually they were married. Their relationship was close, and she could no longer imagine a sexual relationship with anyone else. For a time these uncontrolled perversions seemed to dissipate. She kept their marriage sacred and never committed adultery or anything like that, but ultimately she was still bound to sexual imaginations and compulsive sexual behavior. She felt controlled like a puppet on a string by these evil spirits. Not yet a Christian, she desperately wanted to be free and called out to the Lord. Shortly thereafter, she and her husband both became Christians, and she began to pray to God that this evil compulsion would be removed from her life.

She tells her story about how the control of her "Babylonian" captivity was completely taken out of her life. I love her story because she literally walked out a self-deliverance. So many people receive prayer, deliverance, laying on of hands, and prophetic impartation, but they still go back to their bondage. I believe there are principles from her story that every person can apply in removing the spirit of Babylon. There were three key things she did that caused every evil spirit to lose its hold, and that reprogrammed her pattern of living.

1. She prayed regularly and asked the Lord to remove every wrong desire.

2. She was honest and opened up to her husband about her present compulsive behavior even though her extensive sexual past was no secret to him.

3. She asked the Lord to give her the proper sexual desires toward her husband.

Do you know what the Lord did for her? First, He removed all sexual desire from her. Literally, all of it! She didn't care about sex at all anymore. Now, ultimately that will destroy a marriage, but she believes today that this short season was necessary because God wanted her to start over with a clean slate. Some old things had to be taken out so something new could be planted by the Lord. The Lord was supernaturally reprogramming her mind. God had answered part one of her prayer. The compulsions were completely gone.

However, God wasn't done yet. Her openness about the entire thing with her husband exposed her captivity to the spirit of Babylon. So, lastly, the Lord literally rebuilt a proper sexual desire in her for her husband.

You see, this woman learned to destroy the spirit of Babylon because she saw it, admitted to it, and then with the Lord's help removed it. She was tired of the distress left behind from the devil's invasion. She and her husband have a wonderful marriage today, and they serve the Lord together with all their hearts. As far as they are concerned, they feel as if there has never been a sexual relationship with anyone else. They testify that God can do the impossible and truly make you pure from the past that Babylon has left behind. Isn't that powerful?

> Consistent prayer will arm you to tear down strongholds and allow God to deal with you.

Here's a quick review, or more of a short teaching, on the key biblical principles she applied to destroy her area of Babylon. It will help you in your purpose of defeating your Babylon.

Prayer

Ask God to change you and help you remove all captivity. Don't be afraid to discuss your problem areas with the Lord. Consistent prayer will arm you to tear down strongholds and allow God to deal with you. Jesus taught this principle to His disciples in the Garden of Gethsemane when He said to them, "Why sleep ye? rise and pray, lest ye enter into temptation" (Luke 22:46).

Jesus wanted them to be armed with prayer so they could successfully overcome the pressure arising from the events just around the corner. Unfortunately they slept instead and ended up in trouble during a time of temptation. Prayer will change you.

Confession

You can't live your life hiding your faults from everyone. Now, that does not mean you have to tell everyone you know about your sins. Not everyone can handle certain information about some things, and it will do more harm than good. Your closest friends, family, or pastor, however, should hopefully be safe to expose your captivity and create accountability to no matter how large or small the issue.

If it plagues you and you want to be rid of it, then confide in a mature believer you can trust. James 5:16 says, "Confess your faults one to another, and pray one for another, that ye may be healed." There is healing that comes with being honest about what is plaguing your life.

Submission

This means you submit to God. We do that by taking the time to allow Him to impart a new way of life in us. It comes by reading God's Word and staying around things that will impart righteousness into our lives even when we might not want to do that. We must choose to read the Bible, go to church often, and get involved with other strong believers. We also have to watch everything that we see and hear. Start filling up with the things of the Spirit. That is what submission to God is all about.

Galatians 5:16 says, "This I say then, Walk in the Spirit, and ye shall not fulfil the lust of the flesh." In other words, do spiritual things regularly, and suddenly you won't desire fleshly things as you once did. That is how you submit to God and allow His power to change you supernaturally.

BLUEPRINT STEP #2:
Find Your Post

This part of the plan is so important because most people who have forged through a lot in their lives usually come away feeling a lost sense of direction. That is why the devil tampers with you! He wants to keep you feeling like a slave to your situation so that you are no use to God or anyone else. Captivity does one major thing: it keeps its victims feeling like they are good for nothing, so they do nothing but serve their circumstances. If you want to rise up from the past, you must find a purpose in life other than doing damage control.

Finding or just reclaiming your purpose in life is easier than we think. We can locate it in one simple beginning statement. Find your purpose by asking yourself one question: "What can I not live without?" In other words, what is the direction in your life that you cannot get away from?

You see, I didn't receive an open vision about my calling into ministry. All I ever received was a moment when I went to a large ministry meeting in a convention center. I saw a well-known woman preacher ministering and said to myself, "I want to do that." Except for that, all my other circumstances seemed to tell me to forget the whole idea. I had nothing to go on except something deep down inside me that drove me toward it. Early on, I didn't have a prophecy or anyone to mentor me. There was no one who could teach me how to get it done. I didn't have any money for Bible school. I just knew becoming a preacher of God's Word was the thing I could not live without. There seemed to be no avenue for getting there, but it never left me. As a teenager I "played preacher" all alone in my

> Captivity keeps its victims feeling like they are good for nothing, so they do nothing but serve their circumstances.

bedroom. I listened to teaching tapes and imagined myself preaching like the ministers on the tapes. I set up an ironing board as my pulpit and practiced in my mirror. No one knew it, but it was what I loved and dreamed about. Finding your post begins with putting your finger on the thing that burns in your heart the most.

Give Me That Wall or Give Me Death (I Think)

Now, Nehemiah wanted to build that wall very much, or so he thought. After he decided for sure this was what he wanted to do, he looked things over and decided to move forward. Even knowing the severity of the situation, he was still determined. That decision from him would be tested with the same test every Christian must pass if they want to be sure about their calling in life. It is the test that you find yourself willing to go out on a limb for it. It is the moment when you cross the line and say, "Give me my purpose for God, or nothing!"

Nehemiah quickly discovered that this purpose of wall building ran so deep inside him that he would have died for the cause of it. Those who worked with him had to find the same determination. Now, that doesn't always mean we die a literal death to carry out our purpose, but there are certainly going to be some things that we will have to sacrifice.

Along with Nehemiah, however, was a group of people who only wanted to work for the rebuilding of the wall as long as it didn't require too much of them. Nehemiah 3:5 says, "But their nobles put not their necks to the work of their Lord." In other words, they wanted the benefit of it but without any work. That test determined what was really important to them.

Too many people today want things easily. You have heard it before. We live in a microwave, drive-through society. We want everything now. We like microwave popcorn in three minutes or less, and with no pan to clean up. We like one-stop shopping in a superstore. We've come to expect drive-through banking, ATMs, restaurants, drugstores, and coffee shops. I even found out recently that one city has a morgue that offers drive-through visitation. It's true! We want service now.

> If you are not willing to sacrifice dearly for something, then you probably aren't in love with it or called to it.

Personally, I feel like I have lost precious time if my computer takes longer than five seconds to change screens.

We also see today many infomercials that offer easy jobs with little training and big payouts. Somehow I don't think God works like that. Actually, we don't really find anywhere that He is a God of convenience. Instead we discover that He is a God of sacrifice. If you are not willing to sacrifice dearly for something, then you probably aren't in love with it or called to it. For example, if you truly feel called to become a doctor, then you will sacrifice the time to attend college for the next ten to twelve years. It may cost you a lot of money and countless hours as you put most of your leisure time on hold. In fact, in that profession you may find very little leisure time in life ever again. Yet because your heart burns for it, you will do whatever it takes.

When we started our church, we put everything we had on the line for it. We took out credit in our name to make the ministry happen. If the church closed its doors, we would have been personally left with a lot of debt. We put in countless hours of planning, working, painting, and then, of course, the preaching. We did everything imaginable. I typed the bulletin and preached the sermon. My husband painted the nursery and preached the sermon.

I remember putting together our first church bookstore. I went to a local superstore, bought some bookshelves, piled them in my car, and set them up for Sunday, completely decorated with books and some fake flowers and grapes. Actually it resembled more of a "book area" than a bookstore. It was right out in the open, in the back of the "sort-of sanctuary" at the time. That is because our entire building was one room, like a studio apartment, with areas specified for different things. We had a "sanctuary area," a "book area," and a "foyer area," all from which you could see the pulpit. Then there was one room off the back for the "children's department." Everyone wore so many hats we could have opened a hat store.

Actually, that hasn't changed too much, even though we don't personally type the bulletin anymore because there is staff who does it now. Yet to this day, we both will do whatever it takes and wear whatever hat is necessary. That is why I don't like it when Christians and church people are so opinionated about pastors. Everyone wants to determine what pastors should and should not do, but they don't see all the days and nights they stayed awake finding a way to make the ministries happen. They don't know how they put themselves, their families, and their finances on the line to birth the will of God. Those same people who have big opinions about the pastors determine for themselves if, when, and how often they want to attend services, tithe, or serve in the church. Remember that most ministers are good-hearted and probably died a thousand deaths before they came preaching to you on Sunday. Be a loving support to them because it is likely you don't know the price they pay behind the scenes.

We knew God called us to start a church because it burned in our hearts and we would have done anything for it. We were willing to work countless hours, forge through people's opinions, and give our lives to its success. To this day, I still love workdays at the church. I always want to roll up my sleeves and get in and be a part of them even though I can't do it as often as I used to.

You know you have found your call when neither man nor beast can throw you off it. You will keep coming back after a multitude of tests, trials, and discouraging circumstances. In Romans 16:4, Paul commended Aquila and Priscilla for putting themselves on the line when he said, "Who have for my life laid down their own necks: unto whom not only I give thanks, but also all the churches of the Gentiles." These two incredible teachers of the Word found their post in supporting the ministry of Paul. They were willing to take risks to do it for the long haul.

Ask yourself what you are willing to take a risk to pursue because you know that no matter what, you just have to fulfill that purpose. If you aren't willing to put time and money into it over many years, then it's probably not your ultimate destiny.

It's About the Kingdom

As you find your purpose in life, remember that it is not just about you, but everything we do in life involves the kingdom of God. Your short-term and long-term goals should always have a benefit for the kingdom. Everyone has skills that can be of special benefit to the church. For example, if you are a lawyer, then your services and skills should also benefit and help the church. If you are an artist, then use your talents for the Lord's work. Our talents and plans must always further the work of God and His church. Certainly your money should support the kingdom.

Without a kingdom priority, we leave our purpose open to be tampered with again by the devil. On the other hand, you will only

> Reclaiming and building your purpose in life begins with knowing that you cannot do it alone. The Lord has to build it.

enhance your purpose in life by making the kingdom of God a priority. Like Psalm 69:9 says, "The zeal of thine house hath eaten me up." We have to have a zeal for His house. And when you are consumed with God's purposes, He will help you in yours.

BLUEPRINT STEP #3:
Build Your House

Now, building your dream house doesn't happen overnight. Most people don't move into the house of their dreams right after they leave their parents' house. The process usually starts with that small apartment, then to a starter house, then to a better house or two, and then, ultimately, your dream-house day finally arrives. The first key to reclaiming and building your purpose in life begins with knowing that you cannot do it alone. The Lord has to build it.

We know the familiar scripture that says, "Except the LORD build the house, they labor in vain that build it" (Ps. 127:1). Of course, this does not mean that we can sit back, eat pizza, and do nothing because "the Lord is building the house." What it means is that while you build, the Lord will be the general contractor in charge of the project. This also means that He may temporarily interrupt your building plans in order to adjust your work ethic. He may change your schedule, move the job site, spend some money, or ask you to add some special new materials. He can do whatever He wants, when He wants. Oh, yes! As the general contractor, He may do it when you don't expect it and when it is the least convenient for you. Following Him through it is a process, but it will always build your spiritual dream house in the end.

Once God has established inside you what your purpose in life is supposed to be, then it's time to follow Him and build it. In fact, it's not an option—God expects you to build something with your life! You are commanded by God to leave a powerful mark on Planet Earth. Part of the anointing on King Cyrus was to build a work for God. Ezra 1:2 says, "…The LORD God of heaven…hath charged me to build him an house.…" Now, to be charged with something is very serious. It means you are commanded to do it. Coming out of captivity means you must accomplish something significant.

Now, that does not mean you have to become a world-renowned leader, build the latest innovations in technology, or win a Nobel Prize. God just expects everyone to do something unique and special for Him. It starts by taking a life that was once a mess and making it a praise to His name. Then it involves helping His kingdom in some way. Maybe it means becoming the best Sunday school teacher you can be, or the most joyful and dependable parking lot attendant at the church. There are numerous things it involves, but the important thing is to be a builder and build something with the life God has given you.

> It's not an option—
> God expects you
> to build something
> with your life!

Read the Instructions for Building

Everyone has bought furniture or some other item that comes with those little words on the box stating "ready to assemble." *Uh huh!* Surely, you can remember an experience with one of those. Then when there were some unexpected parts left over, you found yourself saying, "Yes, but it was those faulty directions. I didn't understand them."

In some cases, you just chose to bypass the instruction sheet altogether! We find a short instruction sheet in Ezra 1 that the people used to come out of their captivity and begin an active rebuilding process. This is the part so many people miss. You cannot have effective deliverance without active progress. In other words, for your freedom from bondage to become rooted and secure, you need to be actively planting something to replace the old habits and patterns. That is why building for God is so important in your life. Ask yourself, "What has God called me to accomplish?" Then develop the game plan to get started. You can begin with Ezra's simple instructions.

Rise up!

> Then rose up the chief of the fathers...whose spirit God had raised, to go up to build...
>
> —Ezra 1:5

You have to rise up and move toward your dream. Ask God to open doors and give you direction, but His word to you is "begin." That doesn't mean you have to take giant steps; begin with small steps. We started our first ministry office by putting a desk in a spare room.

If you know that the thing God wants you to build right now will replace some old habit, then decide what things you can add to your schedule in place of it. For example, if you are trying to quit smoking, then replace the times you smoked a cigarette with something godly and positive. If you are trying to overcome anger, then pinpoint the situations that used to get you steamed up before they arise, and prepare an action plan for the next time a similar situation happens. The key is not to sit there every day wondering if you really have changed or if something is going to work out. Instead, rise up today and start building.

Strengthen your hands.

> And all they that were about them strengthened their hands...
>
> —Ezra 1:6

This means you need to start collecting tools and supplies. For some there is schooling needed in order to strengthen their hands. For others it may require changing some financial habits. Collecting the right supplies may not happen in one day, but begin developing the things in your life that will empower you and educate you toward your destiny.

Notice for the people in Ezra it involved them giving and offering themselves. Strengthening your hands may mean you have to sow an offering or give your time. It might mean practice to become good at something. Strengthening involves instruction and training. Become a specialist at what God has put in your heart. Learn by practice, so you can be strong and good at whatever it is that you do.

Connect to God's house.

> Also Cyrus the king brought forth vessels of the house of the Lord, which Nebuchadnezzar had brought forth out of Jerusalem...
>
> —Ezra 1:7

Whenever people are living with bondage in their life, they always seem to disconnect from church and God's people. When people are struggling, church is usually first on the list of things to cut from their lives. If you want to keep your building process fresh and alive, your vision must stay connected with the kingdom. That means you cannot be a loner or only develop relationships with your own "predetermined select few."

Find a good church in your area and connect with people who pray, love God, and support their pastors. Then get involved helping the vision of that ministry. Use your talents to support it because your house will be built when you commit to build God's house. That is God's way because we are all vessels designed to be a blessing to His work.

BLUEPRINT #4:
Restore Your Heritage

This is a last and important part of reclaiming your purpose in life. I like to think of it like a refrigerator again. Have you ever noticed that when you clean out the fridge to prepare it for new groceries, it is never a onetime process? I wish it were! Every week it seems like something that used to be food turns into a creepy science project. Something spills, while something else goes stale and has to be refreshed. Then if we leave it there, suddenly you find you have a full refrigerator but nothing to eat.

I know something is wrong when the kids start saying, "Mom, there's nothing to eat," while I am saying to myself, "I thought there were lots of things in the fridge." No, in reality, the fridge was being used for nothing but storing quickly rotting leftovers. Then after I clean them out, it is amazing how empty it becomes. This process of filling, clean out, and then refilling is necessary if you are going to use the refrigerator for its intended purpose. On a regular basis, it has to be restored to its rightful place.

To keep our purpose for God fresh, we have to live aware that God wants to keep refreshing our vision, our direction, and our heritage. This process is called restoration. Without it we easily get off focus and start putting our lives to use for something God did not intend. Then we are always left with rotten leftovers. And before too long we realize we have not left a good heritage for others to come along later and enjoy.

Nehemiah had to help the people through the process of restoration while he was building the wall of Jerusalem. In Nehemiah 5, the people began to cry in frustration because they realized that even though their captivity was being broken and something wonderful was taking place, they still had not been enjoying what was rightfully theirs. Their captors had still been slyly holding their belongings under control. Sure, God was bringing them from bondage and rebuilding the wall, but what were they going to leave for their children?

To reclaim what rightfully belonged to the people, Nehemiah had to take authority. In Nehemiah 5:7 he rebuked the nobles. Do you know that if you want the promises God has given you to be present, you will need to command them to be upon you? Otherwise the devil will try to steal them. Even though they are yours as God's inheritance, the thief will try to take them away without you realizing it (John 10:10). Then while you think you have built a great work in your life for God, you wake up one day to nothing but leftovers.

Nehemiah took authority by command when he said, "Restore, I pray you, to them, even this day, their lands, their vineyards, their oliveyards, and their houses, also the hundredth part of the money, and of the corn, the wine, and the oil, that ye exact of them" (Neh. 5:11). Then do you know what happened in verse 12? The nobles who had been stealing their heritage gave back what already belonged to them!

To build and reclaim your sense of purpose in life and for God, you will have to stand up for what God has promised you. Don't let the devil take it away so easily. Decide you want your promises to manifest and command them to be yours, just as Nehemiah did. After all, God gave them to you, right? On a regular basis, you must command your rightful heritage to be restored. If not, you will wake up one day and find yourself doing without some wonderful things God wants to be present in your life. You will be working hard for God but living outside His best. Reclaim your right to be healed. Stand up and expect to prosper. If you need peace of mind, claim what God has promised you regarding peace. It's your heritage; don't let the devil replace it with rotten leftovers.

What are the things that your years of captivity in Babylon stole away from you? Did it steal your joy? Did it take your family happiness? Maybe it stole your houses and finances. Command what belongs to you to be restored. You have the right to take them back and enjoy them. Doing so will cause your sense of purpose to rise up with fresh power!

When he gave to the sea his decree, that the waters should not pass his commandment: when he appointed the foundations of the earth: Then I was by him, as one brought up with him: and I was daily his delight, rejoicing always before him.

[PROVERBS 8:29-30]

CHAPTER 8

The KING'S DECREE KEEPS YOUR LIFE on COURSE

P RAY FOR EYES" WAS THE WORD I HEARD SPOKEN SO POWER-
fully to my spirit during my time of prayer. I was seeking the
Lord about a particular meeting in which I would be ministering and wanted to get the mind of God for it. I could not get
away from that fact that I knew the Holy Spirit wanted me to pray
for people with various eye conditions. The words *nearsightedness,
cataracts, astigmatism, blindness,* and *glaucoma* all came to mind. The
Lord definitely had a planned agenda. I prayed about it and expected
the Lord to do many miracles for people with eye conditions.

During the meeting, I preached and then ended the meeting with
a time of ministry. I called for people with eye conditions. The presence of the Lord was in the room, and people were ready to receive
from God. I could literally feel the atmosphere of miracles. When
possible, I like to lay my hands on people to impart miracles for
healing because the Lord uses me that way more often than other
ways. When the call was made, people came to the front with eye
conditions. God moved on people and many were blessed.

In particular, I called for people to be healed of glaucoma. Now,
if you know anything about this particular condition, you know it is
very serious. It causes excess eye fluid, generally in older adults, that
ultimately causes blindness. You have to have confidence in the Lord

to pray for people who have it. However, nothing is impossible for the power of God. Nothing! I expect God to heal people no matter what is wrong with them. To God, glaucoma is no different than a headache.

As I prayed for people's eyes, I began to ask different ones if they noticed a physical manifestation of any sort. I was determined to see miracles, and I knew what God had said to me. I wanted to know what was happening to them right then so we could all rejoice together. And people reported actually feeling different things, such as a burning sensation or a change in their eyes. They were excited.

Yet there was one man in the line who really affected me in a negative way. In fact, he stood right in the middle of the line where it was obvious for everyone to see. I asked him, "Sir, do you feel anything happening to you?" Now others had responded to the same question with a joyful yes, and many had fallen on the floor touched by the power of God. Not this man. When I asked him if he felt God touching him, he stood there like a statue and spoke loudly with a firm and direct, "No!" Everyone could hear him too. It was kind of embarrassing. I encouraged him to believe the Lord for a miracle and went on to others.

Coming back to him, I would ask the same questions. I asked him if he felt any kind of touch from God, a presence, or a sensation of any sort on his body. Each time he responded with the same immediate, loud, and almost resistant, "No!" No voice tone change, no sense of emotion, just "No!"

Finally after many attempts, I moved on and decided it was best not to continue working with him. The sad part was that God was ministering in so many ways, but the man just couldn't get in the river of the Holy Spirit. He wasn't even willing to try.

For some reason that event really tampered with me. It is amazing how you can witness five or ten miracles, and the one that didn't work out is the one that wants to dominate your thinking. Certainly the devil was trying to use that situation to break down my confidence in praying for the blind or other serious outward conditions such as deafness or even crippled people. Of course, I have encountered many people who had trouble receiving a miracle or maybe didn't feel anything right at the moment, but this man almost seemed as if he wanted to prove a point. In any case, determined to resist the mental attack, I didn't give it too much thought.

A few months later I was preparing to minister in another meeting and began to get that sense that the Lord was going to talk to me again about eyes. Please! Now the Lord didn't really say it exactly, but I had that feeling. You know when your spirit starts to focus on something during prayer, and you can't help but get the sense that God wants to focus in a particular direction. I knew the witness of the Holy Spirit was building inside me for eyes again. While going about daily business, I can almost remember saying in my head in that singsong, childish tone, "Lord, I can't hear You. I won't do that. No, I won't." I told myself, "I will preach, I will prophesy to a couple of people, and that's it. No eyes!"

Then just prior to the meeting, my husband casually mentioned to me in passing, "Hey, when you minister in the meeting, the Lord says be sensitive to pray for eyes."

What? I could have lashed out irrationally! Instead, I smiled curtly at my main man and said, "Sure, dear."

OK, now this is where you have to decide between what God *said* and what it was that you really wanted to *hear*. I wanted to hear, "Preach a powerful sermon that will change lives." God didn't have a problem with that, but He had something else on His mind. Personally, I felt that I *needed* to go along with what made me feel safe and confident, not by what God—or even my husband—said about it . . . *humph!*

I went and preached the meeting. Now I do know better than to completely defy God's directions, so I did call for eyes. Honestly, I didn't call for prayer in a way that I laid hands on individuals, but

I called a group of people and prayed one corporate prayer for them. It was nice and safe. Anyhow, it seemed God ministered to people even though I didn't call out anyone in particular. Thank the Lord He helps us in spite of ourselves. God was teaching me, however, to stay with what He *said* over what made me feel comfortable.

Then, several months later, someone in our church had suffered a fairly serious foot injury right in our own church building just before service began. Actually, the accident was serious enough to require a fairly involved surgery. We knew it was an attack, but the event tried to work on the minds of both my husband and me because this interference happened at our church. Days later, while again preparing for a conference, I heard the Spirit say, "You will pray for injuries, ligaments, arthritis, and problems with limbs."

God, please! Have you ever noticed that it seems God asks a lot of you right at the moment you feel the most challenged? He always expects you to immediately confront the thing that messes with you. I have also noticed that the Lord is not always understanding with where you're at emotionally at the time. He doesn't wait until you muster your own confidence about something. After a serious limb injury right on our church property, I have to go out and pray for injured and crippled people. Gracious!

Once again, this is when you have to decide if you will run with what God *said* or if you will adapt it to what you are experiencing. This time, I furthered my determination and called out a lady, telling her that she had been injured the day before (I knew in my heart it was in her legs, but I didn't say it right away). I told her to come forward because God wanted her to know that this attack of the devil was unacceptable.

Then I called out arthritis and other problems. People came to the front and suddenly began to manifest their miracles. Injured people were jumping, lifting up walking canes, and similar movements. One lady handed me an adverse doctor's report about her back that she was believing God to heal. She came to the meeting with the problem, but you could clearly see she was healed that day. Another lady, from that same event, wrote our ministry later and said she felt a supernatural tingling in her hands for days after. She was completely healed of arthritis. Thank God!

> Forgetting the Word of the Lord is the primary reason people's lives get off course again and again.

I realized that *the power was not in staying with what I felt safe to do but with what the Lord said to do.* Since all of this, I have seen the Lord do countless miracles with eyes, legs, and many other conditions because I stayed with what God said. The power is in the King's decree!

A Search Has to Be Made

Let's think back again at all the challenges that Israel faced when both Ezra and Nehemiah began to reclaim their purpose after many long years of captivity. They could have easily reverted back to following the thing that felt safe instead of what God actually intended and decreed for them. In fact, this is one of the biggest challenges for every Christian. It is the reason people backslide, give up on their miracles, stop tithing, get divorced, quit going to church, or even quit serving God altogether. They get off course when they are put under pressure because they forget, or have trouble remembering, what God said to them. During a trial or moment of frustration, they forget what they read in the Bible, or after a disappointment they no longer bring to mind the prophetic word they received.

It seems as though, when we get tampered with, one of the first things to go out the window is the Word of the Lord. *Forgetting the Word of the Lord is the primary reason people's lives get off course again and again.* Because of this tendency, we have to know how to hold on to the things we have heard God say so our purpose for Him stays right on target. If there is any lesson or any truth to be learned in this book, this one is probably the most pivotal of all.

In the Book of Ezra, while God's people were busy and excitedly rebuilding the temple under some of the most hellacious attacks, they did something very specific that kept them on course with the project. In Ezra 5, their adversaries had questioned whether they had the right or authority to do the work. The elders overseeing the work answered their adversaries with a powerful comeback: "In the first year of Cyrus the king of Babylon the same king Cyrus *made a decree to build this house of God*" (Ezra 5:13, emphasis added).

What did the king make? He made a decree. That means he *said* something that he, as the supreme authority, expected to be honored and carried out. There were adversaries, however, who questioned what he had said. They questioned the king's decree.

Notice what the elders did after the word of the king was called into question. They didn't fall apart because this was the last straw. Realize they had been under repeated attacks. The work had been resisted, frustrated, and halted even to the point where it couldn't get going again during the reign of the very king who first told them to do it. You see, so many of us give up when the heat is on at that level. Yet they did one thing. They would not relent with what King Cyrus had decreed. Under tremendous pressure to change what they knew to be true, they went to the current king, Darius, and said, "...let there be search made in the king's treasure house, which is there at Babylon, whether it be so, that a decree was made of Cyrus the king to build this house of God..." (v. 17).

What did they do? They went back and researched what King Cyrus actually said. Pressure and negative circumstances, combined with people's opinions and disagreements, can cause you to become cloudy with the thing God told you. Trials can make you forget the truth of the Scriptures. Then the temptation is to change directions or change what you believe because you can't handle the resistance. In this case the elders of Israel were able to hold on to the decree that came from the king because they went back and searched out what was said. They couldn't just try to *remember*; they had to go back and search it out, even though they knew the general idea of the king's decree.

How often do we know the general idea of a prophetic word we received or a biblical truth

> It is just too risky and easy to change Bible truth to fit our circumstances, especially during a trial.

we once studied? Perhaps you spent the week reading Bible verses on overcoming fear, but after a period of time, when a fearful situation really intimidated you, you forgot to apply what you read. We can all remember times when this has happened.

So the builders of the temple did a review of the king's decree, but did you happen to notice where they went in order to do that review? They went to the king's treasure house. This was the designated place where all the king's laws, decrees, and commandments were archived. For us, King Jesus has designated treasure houses in the spirit where we can go and review what He has decreed over our lives. The first and most obvious treasure house of the King's decrees is the Bible.

You have probably heard the statement: *if you want to know the will of God, read the Word of God*. Depending on what you are standing for in your life, you will need to make a regular search and review of Scripture. Often you will be reviewing the same scriptures again and again. Never think you have gone over the same verses too many times. You have to keep reviewing the Lord's decree for your situation from His treasure house of Scripture. It is just too risky and easy to change Bible truth to fit our circumstances, especially during a trial. Go to the King's treasure house and repeatedly review

His written Word so you know what you believe even under pressure and persecution.

> Good, biblical instruction will keep you heading toward the things the Lord is saying instead of allowing you to be sidetracked.

Another place we can find the decree of the Lord in His treasure house is through the prophetic word. That is through personal prophecy, prophecies to the church, or even words the Holy Spirit puts in our own hearts through revelation. We need this type of decree because without it we get religious and lifeless. Truths of the Bible coupled with the sound prophetic Word of the Lord are extremely powerful. The apostle Paul reminded Timothy, "...according to the prophecies which went before on thee, that thou by them mightest war a good warfare" (1 Tim. 1:18).

The prophetic word in you can be a weapon as long as you don't forget about it. You can war with those words by writing them down, reviewing them, and meditating on them. Keep searching that treasure house. Think over what the Lord is trying to tell you in that word. Declare it and repeat it aloud just as you would the scriptures you are standing on.

I often keep certain personal words I have received in my Bible so I can keep my spirit filled with them. Then when a situation arises that tells me the very opposite of that word, I am armed to stand up for what the King has already decreed for me.

Lastly, remember the King's treasure house contains a wealth of His powerful decrees. Those decrees are also found spoken, repeated, and prayed *at church*. By just attending a strong and anointed local church, you will find the King's decree for your life manifesting all around you. Regular contact and fellowship with on-fire believers will open to you a treasure in the spirit. Good, biblical instruction will keep you heading toward the things the Lord is saying instead of allowing you to be sidetracked by whatever might be going on with you personally or with your family.

Where Are the Garbage Bags?

Of course, if you have raised a family—especially if you have raised teenagers—you automatically know that food is a big part of your life. By now, our household should have owned stock in every potato chip company in the country. I think the door to our refrigerator spends more time open than closed. And I have decided that the largest part of our grocery shopping consists of kids' snack items, especially beverages. Thank the Lord we graduated from a broken-down refrigerator to a much better one!

We finally came to a point, however, where one fridge wasn't doing the trick. The bottled water, juice, and containers of soda were taking over. So there came a day when we bought a second one and put it in the family room. Now we have two of them to fill.

So you can imagine what grocery day is like for our family. It is almost embarrassing! My husband and I go together and pile up two carts—he can perfectly arrange more groceries into a cart than anyone I have ever met. I just know the cashiers want to run away when they see us coming.

After we get home, we have the grueling process of unloading and putting everything away. Oh, it takes a long time. Then as we are rummaging through all the sacks, my spouse and shopping cohort says something like, "Dear, did you find the garbage bags yet?"

Then I stop, completely still, and think, "No, it can't be. The garbage bags. How could I have forgotten to buy garbage bags? It was the most important item, the main reason we went to the store. I can't believe I didn't buy garbage bags!"

Has this ever happened to you? Just about that time, you look around the kitchen and see the trash piling up, groceries everywhere, dishes in the dishwasher, and mounting chaos—but no trash bags anywhere, not one. So you ask yourself, "How is it that I just bought out the entire store but didn't buy the most important item on my...list? Oh, yeah, the list—the one that was in my head. If only I *had* made a list, I wouldn't have forgotten the garbage bags!" Then, unsure of what to do with the mounting trash created by the groceries being put away, you use whatever is around—grocery sacks, an old dry cleaning bag—because you certainly aren't going back out to the store now.

We are so often the same way in the things of the spirit. We try to commit everything the Lord says to memory. Now the memorization of God's Word *is* a wonderful thing. I believe the reason God wrote His Word down in the pages of the Bible, however, is because the Lord knows we cannot possibly recall His lists and lists of promises and commandments when chaos is happening everywhere. Just like on grocery day, you cannot possibly remember everything from your head. In fact, the greater the trial or test, the more imperative it is that you have a written decree from God in your hand. If not, you will find yourself forgetting something that you desperately need—a life-changing promise, a key commandment, or an important directive. Sometimes we don't actually forget what the Lord said; we just change it slightly because, in light of our present situation, His promises or commandments might feel too extreme. During these times, we are tempted to veer off course in the spirit as we try to create quick solutions and shortcuts to the problem at hand.

As a pastor, I always have opportunities to give people spiritual guidance about problems in their life. I don't try to be a professional counselor. My job as a minister of the gospel is to remind people of what the Lord has said. That is how I deal with myself. I have found in giving "counsel" to myself that if I just redirect my attention back to what the Lord has already spoken or decreed, there is always plenty of good counsel there.

People have said to me, however, "Pastor Brenda, I can appreciate what you are saying, but I don't think you understand the severity of my problem or where I am coming from."

They may be right; I probably don't. But the Lord does! That is why He gave us the Bible. He always has answers, and He has probably already shown plenty of them to you. I don't think the Lord forgot to place the right counsel in His Word relevant to your problem. Yet when people are convinced their problem is too severe for the Bible or even the prophetic word they received, they almost always look for help elsewhere. In fact, I have talked to people, giving them counsel right from the Bible, and then later they will write me a letter saying, "Thanks for the help, but I really need other professional counseling instead."

> **Before we look for new answers, we need to review and practice the ones we already have in our hands, bound in black leather—the Bible!**

Now please don't misunderstand what I am saying. I am not against good Christian counselors. My trouble is that each time someone has said that to me, I can almost always see where they are already ignoring or not practicing the Word of the Lord—the Bible. Before we keep looking for new answers, we need to review and practice the ones we already have in our hands, bound in black leather! Imagine how the need for marriage counseling would be reduced if we would just put to practice the scriptures about love, watching our words, and mortifying the deeds of the flesh. It's hard to keep fighting and mistreating one another when we make a firm determination to do what God has already said. I should think that two Christians in a marriage should be able to do this.

You see, like the elders of Israel, we need to take hold of the

King's decree and keep doing what He has said—no matter how we feel or what pressure we are facing at the moment. You can't just try to remember what you heard preached once or what the prophecy said on Sunday. You have to look at it again and again. If you are having trouble acting lovingly in your marriage, then maybe it requires taking God's decrees about love and carrying these written words around with you for constant reference. Keep searching the King's treasure house. That is how you stay on course in life, and when the enemy is tampering with you, you will not be overcome and change your strategy.

Three Demonic Schemes

The devil doesn't play fairly. Actually, he isn't playing at all. This is real spiritual warfare, and we have to know how to counterattack against our adversary, or else, if we let him, he *will* keep tampering with our lives.

> Satan always has plenty of people lined up who are more than willing to talk you right out of the Word of the Lord. Some of them are very good at it too!

The one thing Satan knows is that if he can get you to question and thus ignore what God has said, he has you. Here I will again mention how he tricked Eve in the garden, asking her, "Hath God said?" (Gen. 3:1). If the devil cannot get you to overlook what God said with a simple question like the one he asked Eve, however, he doesn't mind using mountainous circumstances to test your determination. This is what happened during the rebuilding of the temple when the adversaries of the project launched a campaign to stop the work: "Then the people [adversaries] of the land weakened the hands of the people of Judah, and troubled them in building, and hired counsellors against them, to frustrate their purpose, all the days of Cyrus king of Persia, even until the reign of Darius king of Persia" (Ezra 4:4–5).

Let's look at the three ways their enemies discouraged them from staying on course with the Word of the Lord. I believe they are the very same things the enemy uses to discourage us from holding on to what God has said to us and rebuilding our dreams for God. He uses these same schemes to get us off focus from God's directives so that we can no longer fulfill our destiny.

SCHEME #1: *He weakened the hands of the people.*

Typically, if we get tired enough, we don't want to read the Bible or do much else. Tiredness can be physical, but it can also be mental and emotional. After many trials, the tendency is to get emotionally exhausted, and we can easily find ourselves saying, "I just can't take another letdown."

Exhaustion is the aim of the devil. He wants to keep you so tired and so busy that you eventually stop declaring the Word of God in one or many areas.

SCHEME #2: *He troubled them in building.*

You have probably heard the old saying, "Two steps forward and one step back." We talked in detail throughout chapter 5 about cycles of trouble. Constant trouble is a classic demonic scheme that wants to make you forget God's promises. If you focus long enough on the bad, you can easily forget the good!

Have you ever noticed how, in the heat of a trial, we no longer agree with, remember, or even understand what God said? Sometimes we even change our most trusted doctrines. We once received and defended the Word of the Lord, but now? *Hmm*...now we tell Him, "Lord, I'm not sure I understand what You were trying to say!"

SCHEME #3: *He hired counselors against them.*

Yes, then there are always people. Of course, there is safety with God-fearing people who are committed to the Word of God. There will always be those, however, who feel God's way is too extreme for you. For example, they think if you tithe 10 percent of your income that you have gone off the deep end. They don't care if it's in the Bible or not; they just think you are out of your mind. So they will say things like, "I can't believe you give all that money to the church. If you would quit doing that, you could drive a better car or be able to get out from under those bills!" Then if you are not careful, you will look around at your financial situation, listen to your relatives gossiping about your tithing, and start wondering where you went wrong.

Satan always has plenty of people lined up who are more than willing to talk you right out of the Word of the Lord. Some of them are very good at it too! It always sounds most convincing, but we must, in turn, always go back to what God said, not what people say or believe. There will be times when you will be severely persecuted for it, but nevertheless, learn to be tenacious with the Word of God.

Hold the Decree in Your Hand

It seemed for a period of time that the three schemes used by the adversaries of the temple project had been successful. Let's summarize what we have discussed thus far about the rebuilding of the temple:

- It was never completed during the reign of Cyrus.

- It was attacked so viciously that it did not get finished during the reign of the next two kings (Ezra 4:5–24).

- It didn't get started again until the reign of Darius, but even then, it still didn't happen.

- It only happened when they went back to the king's original decree.

As the rebuilding project got started again, it took a new kind of determination to forge through the onslaught of attacks. The enemies again questioned their right to do the work, and that is when the people decided they had to stand up for what the king had said. In Ezra 6:2 it says there was a record that was *already written*. In that record they found some very specific directives about the rebuilding of the temple. Had they not gone back to that original decree, I am convinced the project would have been aborted once again.

Now I don't know about you, but there are some promises, some dreams, and some expectations in my life that I am not about to let the enemy abort again. What has the Lord told you that you want to see come to pass? If you are determined to see God's purpose fulfilled for your life, it's time to pick up the King's decree and shake it in the face of the enemy. You need to say it aloud so that you can hear yourself saying it. This is especially true if you have spent years saying something negative every time you're under attack.

Psalm 119:50 says, "This is my comfort in my affliction: for thy word hath quickened me." I encourage you to go back and read all of Psalm 119 to remind yourself how important holding on to the Word of God really is. And verse 50 reminds us to rise above trouble through the Word of God, which is the very thing that imparts life to us—nothing else but what the King has already declared.

> The prophetic word over your life is that you *shall* come into divine destiny.

We need to pick up the King's decree. Yes, we need to actually hold it in our hands and then read it again and again—then read it a few more times—so we can align ourselves with God's opinion even when it feels easier to take another approach.

This was exactly what the elders did in order to avoid another interruption of the temple work. They had to finally get that word back out of the closet and declare it to themselves and to their enemies. Avoid another interruption in your life too. Get the Word of the Lord out of the closet, hold it in your hands, and declare the King's decree!

The Sevenfold Decree of the King

We can take the decree of King Cyrus and use it as a pattern to form the rebuilding of our lives in any place they have been attacked. From Ezra 6:3–11, there were seven directives or parts found in the decree that I believe represent what our King Jesus wants to be decreed over us. Let's look over the specifics of the king's decree and begin to expect them to work in your life.

DIRECTIVE #1: *Let the house be built (Ezra 6:3).*

Today the Lord is saying to you, "Let your spiritual house be built; let your dreams for God be built." In other words, God is giving you the divine right and order to go and do something great with your life that will be a great testimony and benefit to the kingdom of God.

The devil might be speaking great words of defeat to you, but God is saying something else. He is declaring right now, "Let your house be built." If the Lord is saying that, then start expecting and acting like it is true! The prophetic word over your life is that you *shall* come into divine destiny.

DIRECTIVE #2: *Let a strong foundation be laid (Ezra 6:3).*

When God builds something, He does it right. When a building is erected with a proper foundation, it means that it will not crumble easily when things around it begin to shake. A proper foundation is the key to the building's longevity. God is declaring that for you.

What are some of the Christian basics that make a strong foundation? Be consistent in your time with God, pray, read the Bible, and stay close to church and other believers. That is the best place to start or return back to. Start speaking to the foundations of your life. See yourself strong in prayer, see yourself a stable Christian, and expect to be a person who can stand powerfully in the Lord in any situation. *With God's strong foundation in your life, you will not fail.*

> The King is standing before you today, willing to give you whatever you need to make it into your destiny.

DIRECTIVE #3: *Let the expenses be given out of the king's house (Ezra 6:4).*

So often we get the idea that God is not going to provide the resources we need for things. Now, I am not just talking about financial resources—although that is included. What I am talking about is whatever we need God to impart to us so we can build our lives and callings for His glory. Jesus was willing to pay a lot so you can be well supplied for! What He wants you to know is that if you need a miracle in your life, then He will provide one. If you need peace, then He is giving you peace.

We have to be so careful that we don't get tempted to believe we are just muddling through on our own. No! The King is standing before you today, willing to give you whatever you need to make it into your destiny. Start expecting that, because every resource imaginable is available in the King's house.

DIRECTIVE #4: *Restore the silver and gold vessels of the house of God (Ezra 6:5).*

These vessels were the precious instruments of worship that Nebuchadnezzar had stolen. They were the tools that helped the priests fulfill their service to God. When something happens to interfere or tamper with you, it always tries to steal your anointing. These vessels represent the tangible power of God to help us accomplish our service for Him.

When you face opposition, however, it wants to make you struggle to sense the presence of God operating in your life. Know that the King's decree is declaring it to be restored. Instead of fearing that the supernatural will not manifest, start expecting God to give you the spiritual tools (vessels of worship) so you can stand against the enemy in His power. Expect to feel His hand on your life. Expect the gifts of the Spirit to operate in your life, and know that God is providing you with the right tools in order to get the job done.

DIRECTIVE #5: *The adversaries must be removed (Ezra 6:6).*

King Cyrus had commanded that the enemies of the project were not supposed to interfere with the work. In fact, the decree stated they were to be positioned far away. Of course, they interfered anyhow. It was not until the people stood up for the king's command that they overcame and removed their adversaries.

The devil will try to interfere. But be confident; God has decreed that he is not allowed to enter your domain to stop your work for Him. The way to get the devil to run from your territory is to resist him with the King's command—what He has already said. James 4:7 says, "Resist the devil, and he will flee from you." The King has declared that your adversaries have to go!

DIRECTIVE #6: *Daily provision of the sacrifices for worship will be made (Ezra 6:9).*

The king had commanded the people that they should be given daily provisions so they could make their sacrifices of worship. Sometimes when we face things, we don't feel like we want to worship God. Instead, we want to cry or get angry or feel fearful. Truthfully, worship feels like a sacrifice. That is why the Bible refers to praise as a sacrifice sometimes, but there is a blessing when we choose to make that sacrifice.

Jeremiah 33:11 says, "…and of them that shall bring the sacrifice of praise into the house of the LORD. For I will cause to return the captivity of the land, as at the first, saith the LORD." Wow! Does that mean captivity is literally broken because a sacrifice of praise is offered? Yes! It means that we choose to worship God over the negative circumstance before us, and that causes the spirit of captivity to be broken.

But there is more than that. According to the decree of the king, God is even providing us the sacrifice. In other words, when you don't think you can find the strength to make the sacrifice, He will even refresh you with the ability to worship Him beyond your own strength. This is what the King has declared for you, so start to believe it.

DIRECTIVE #7: *No one can alter the king's decree (Ezra 6:11).*

The people of God found that King Cyrus has said something very powerful here. I believe this statement is truly the icing on the cake. The decree stated that if anyone should attempt to alter what had been written, their own house would be pulled down and left as a dunghill. Further, it stated that the ones who altered it were to be hanged. Pretty bold, huh? This shows us that this king was very serious about what he had written. No one was to be changing it or messing with his decree in any way.

We can also see here that Jesus our King is very serious about what He has said too. He doesn't like it when we change His Word because of our own situation. He doesn't like it when the devil tricks us into letting go of His Word. When God says something, He means it! For example, if He promised you joy, then stop accepting depression instead. Start declaring His decree concerning joy and expect it to manifest for you. Don't get caught up altering the Word of the Lord because of how you feel that day. Stay with it come rain or shine. Altering the Word of God because of circumstances in your life will only tear down your own house. It will further the problem. Stay with what the King has spoken, and your house will be built with great blessing and purpose.

Take every part of this sevenfold decree of the King and expect it to be a part of your daily life. After all, if the King said it, then you can be assured that it is dependable for you. The people of Israel held the decree up before their enemies to read and weep! In fact, after the people of God became tenacious with the decree, Tatnai the governor, along with his co-workers, who had been their most fierce opponents, was forced by the current King Darius to help carry out the decree! Ezra 6:13 says, "...so they did speedily."

They realized that they had better get busy following the written word or their own houses were going to be in big trouble. They realized they were about to be hanged because the written decree had been brought back into focus. I believe when you hold up the King's decree, no matter what, you not only build up your own house, but you also tear down the strong house of your enemy the devil. He truly has no power to stand up to what the King has spoken, and he will be forced to retreat.

If there is ever any question in your heart whether the Word of God can be trusted this way, remind yourself of the scripture that was quoted at the beginning of this chapter:

> When he gave to the sea his decree, that the waters should not pass his commandment: when he appointed the foundations of the earth: Then I was by him, as one brought up with him: and I was daily his delight, rejoicing always before him.
>
> —Proverbs 8:29–30

This entire proverb was written about wisdom. It was wisdom, in this verse, that was standing by the Lord when He gave His commandment. Wisdom was the Lord's delight. When God made a permanent decree for nature to be set in motion, wisdom was by Him. In other words, when God makes a permanent order such as boundaries for the oceans, then He only does it as He is guided by His wisdom. That means whatever the Word of God written in the Bible tells you, it will carry sound wisdom that will save your life.

> When you hold up the King's decree, no matter what, you not only build up your own house, but you also tear down the strong house of your enemy the devil.

Now, whatever God has said may sometimes appear crazy to our own thinking. It may look crazy to believe you are healed from arthritis even though you still have pain. Why should you believe you are healed? Because the Lord has decreed it to be so. You can trust that the true way of wisdom is believing what the Lord has said.

What is our proof? The sea has never been able to cross its borders once the Lord told it where its boundaries were. If God's wisdom told the sea what to do, then His wisdom can be trusted for your need as well. You can get your momentum going. Speak the decree of the King so your life can stay on course with the wisdom of the Lord.

Change What Is Set in Motion

Momentum is a powerful thing. As I have mentioned before, one of the old cars we used to own somewhat resembled a tank. It was a big, old luxury car, except that by the time we owned it, it had lost its luxurious appeal. This car housed a V-8 engine and could really move once it got going. We live in a region where there is plenty of snow and ice to go around every winter, and you need a car that works well for that type of weather. This car was not it!

The weight combined with the large front engine and rear-wheel drive made it a monster in the winter. If you have ever driven in icy conditions, you will know that the most difficult part is stopping. That is where most accidents occur. People get going too fast and cannot stop quickly enough on the ice. As a result, you see people careen through intersections or spiral into a ditch. But this old car of ours could get momentum going even when you weren't trying to have any—fifty-five miles an hour felt like you were only going thirty. So I learned that when driving it, I always needed extra time to slow down and stop the momentum, icy or not!

> Whichever one— death or life—we are inclined to love, or to speak the most, that is the one we will live out.

Since we have learned throughout our everyday lives how to deal with our circumstances and problems in a certain way, we will first need to "slow down" and learn a new way of "driving in these icy conditions." We have to learn to handle problems according to the way of the Spirit instead of the flesh. Then we need to realize that when certain negative things have been set in motion for years, sometimes it takes time to reverse the momentum that has been created.

Not everything will turn in one moment, after one prayer, one miracle service, or one prophecy. We have to learn to slow the momentum of evil and turn it into righteousness. This is a process that takes time, but there is a powerful, biblical key: we need to change the momentum of what has been set in motion. Slow the momentum, and you are positioned to reverse the problem.

Proverbs 18:21 says, "Death and life are in the power of the tongue: and they that love it shall eat the fruit thereof." You may have read this verse before, but let's refresh ourselves on what it is saying. It means that we can set death or life in motion based on the things we say. Whichever one—death or life—we are inclined to love, or to speak the most, that is the one we will live out. If we constantly speak the fruit of death, we will eventually eat that fruit. Now, that doesn't just mean physical death. It means defeat, frustrations, fear, anger, and so on. Continually verbalizing our troubles and the things that aggravate us will only feed the problem. On the other hand, verbalizing *life* will cause us to eat the fruit of life.

Notice that the verse says, "...eat the fruit thereof." Fruit takes time to grow. It needs all the right conditions, watering, and nurturing in order to produce. Whatever you are taking the time to nurture with your words is the fruit that is slowly growing in your life. You may not even notice that it is happening because of the process it requires. Your words are continually creating or furthering momentum.

With driving our old car in icy conditions, the best way to slow its momentum was to let off the gas. The first place to reverse the momentum of whatever has tampered with your life is to quit talking about it so much. Let off the gas! Start talking about something else; start speaking about the goodness of God. Start speaking words of grace toward that person you have an offense with. Begin to talk positively about your future. Now, that doesn't mean everything wrong will stop and change in one day, but changing the momentum with a new choice of words will start changing the fruit that has been in motion.

Some people get all upset about the idea of positive speaking and declaring the promises of the Bible, then expecting them to come to pass. They think it is silly to positively talk your way into something. Realize that no one is saying you can command a blue car to turn into a red one, or crazy things like that. I have actually heard preachers mock messages on the power of words and insinuate that people teach that way. No. I am not saying that.

Scripture speaks adamantly about words and what they can impart to our lives over a lifetime. If you don't think words are powerful, think about a time someone you love said something that was hurtful. Words are very powerful because it was words that God used to create the world. We need to make sure our words mimic things that God would say about our lives, our families, and our circumstances.

> The tongue is a fire, a world of iniquity: so is the tongue among our members, that it defileth the whole body, and setteth on fire the course of nature; and it is set on fire of hell.
>
> —James 3:6

That is one confrontational mouthful of truth right there! Actually, you should take the time to read the entire chapter of James 3 on a regular basis. It always helps us keep the things coming from our mouth in check, whether it is about ourselves, our situation, or someone else.

God takes words seriously. See how this verse says we can actually set nature in motion with words. Words can move natural events too. Isn't that what Jesus was doing when He spoke to the storm in Mark 4:39? He commanded the raging storm to be still. Well, you might look at the storm in your life and say, "I have spoken to this storm, and it looks like anything but peaceful and still." Sure, there may still be some raging storms that won't seem to obey when you speak the King's decree over them. Start speaking right, however, and eventually the negative momentum already in motion will begin to change.

In James 3:4, you will see that the Bible likens our tongue to a rudder on a ship: "Sailing ships are driven by strong winds. But a small rudder turns a large ship..." (NLV). But you know, even when a rudder moves a ship it is not an instantaneous movement. Momentum set in motion has to first slow down before something can change course. After the slowing-down process, then the ship gradually changes with the direction of the rudder.

James 3:3 also likens our tongue to the bit in a horse's mouth. Horses will move to the pull of a bit much faster than a ship will respond to a rudder. And the horse is a great example because it has a mind of its own and wants to resist the bit in its mouth. Sometimes it isn't that our words aren't being effective; it is that we are being resisted by the enemy. In both cases, however, the bit and the rudder are powerful. Proper words can change nature set in motion and overcome demonic resistance.

> When you make the wise decision to always speak right and believe what the Lord says, be assured that your destiny will be blessed.

So how does it work? What are we supposed to do? Ephesians 5:19 says, "Speaking to yourselves in psalms and hymns and spiritual songs, singing and making melody in your heart to the Lord." We speak to ourselves. We can actually prophesy the Word of the Lord over our own lives. First, we have to believe what the Lord has said to be the final word. Then we have to put what He says in our mouths and speak it.

When you make the wise decision to always speak right and believe what the Lord says about you, your family, or your situation, be assured that your destiny will be blessed. Take hold of the King's decree no matter what has happened in your life, and you will always find yourself on course!

My meat is to do the will of him that sent me, and to finish his work.

[JOHN 4:34]

[CHAPTER 9]

The ANOINTING to FINISH

THE LIFE OF JESUS WAS ABSOLUTELY AMAZING FOR MANY obvious reasons. Probably one of the most powerful, however, is that our Lord always did everything to completion. He never started anything that He did not finish. All His miracles would not have the same impact had the Lord not finished His work at Calvary. Yet His work at the cross would not have been complete unless He also rose from the grave. To further that, His work was made even more complete through the power of Pentecost and the birthing of the church. So on goes the complete work of Christ through the miracle of salvation and His presence that continually changes our lives.

Throughout this entire book we have discussed in detail the important principles needed in order to rise up again from whatever hardship the devil has thrown our way. We have exposed how the enemy sneaks into our territory and tries to rip the rug out from under us the way he did with Adam and Eve. We can see how the devil's invasion through negative experiences keeps so many bound to captive mind-sets. The blessing is that the same miraculous God of the Bible always has a tailor-made way of bringing us up from the dust and ashes of the past, assuming we put into practice certain principles.

Yet getting started on the right road and even experiencing a few miracles does not mean we will end up in God's best for our lives. We end up in God's best because we finish every spiritual race set before us and never quit. Jesus finished what He started because nothing could make Him give up. It is no different for us. We will experience God's perfect destiny for our lives because we will not give up on the things we start just because it looks like nothing is getting any better.

> Regardless of what you are standing in faith for, there will always be opportunities to give up.

For example, perhaps the devil is tampering with your marriage. This is an important example because so many people express the need for help in their marriages. You may be applying the principles of the Bible and trusting God to restore your relationship. Sometimes, however, there are seasons when you have to continue with endurance until a miracle takes place. Our minds, our lives, and our habits need time for the seed of God's Word to germinate, take root, and produce fruit that remains.

During those seasons, you will always be faced with the decision to either quit standing for your breakthrough or finish what you started in faith and victory. Regardless of what you are standing in faith for—marriage or another issue—there will always be opportunities to give up. At times we can be tempted to give up in some areas of life and not in others. Of course, for every person it seems there are certain areas that will never change. That is where it takes your determination and fortitude.

The most incredible story I know of a person who didn't give up when the circumstances kept tampering with them is the story of Polly Wigglesworth, wife of the famous preacher Smith Wigglesworth. I am sure it has been told by many ministers throughout the years because Polly's husband was famed for his miraculous healing ministry and raising of the dead. As I remember the story, however, the most miraculous part was this woman's determination to see God intervene for her husband's salvation and their marriage.

When the two were married in 1882, Smith was not a practicing Christian. In fact, he was far from it, often being drunk and controlled by demons. Polly's bold and joyful Christianity became an irritant to her husband and was often met with outbursts of anger and violence. But Polly trusted in Acts 16:31, that her entire household—her husband—would be saved if she would just believe. She openly told her husband that she was believing for his salvation, which was often met with beatings if Smith was drunk at the time.

One particular night he threatened against her going to church. In anger he said to her, "If you go to church tonight, when you get home, the doors will be locked!" Undaunted, Polly went off to church. When she came home, the doors were locked! She pounded on them, but Smith did not answer—perhaps he was passed out on the floor. In any case, Polly wrapped herself in the clothes she was wearing and huddled against the house in the cold night air until morning, trusting she would not suffer frostbite.

In the morning, when Smith awoke and realized Polly was not in the house, he went to the door and opened it. Instantly Polly jumped to her feet and said, "Good morning, Smith; are you ready for breakfast?" That incident broke Smith. He instantly gave his life to the Lord and became one of the mightiest ministers of the gospel to walk the earth.

Even if this story has changed or wavered in its telling through the years, you can still see what determination and faith Polly had. She didn't even greet him with a tear because her "feelings were terribly hurt." The whole point is, when Polly's life was tampered with, she stayed with God's promises and never gave up—she never quit believing, trusting God, and expecting a miracle, even though there were many days when it didn't seem anything was changing. She kept extending love and forgiveness mixed with expectancy for the miraculous. And we know this to be true: because she didn't quit, her husband was born again.

What might have happened had she stood up when Smith opened the door that morning to see her screaming in tears, saying, "That's it! I've had enough of your anger and abuse! I am done being mistreated! I'm leaving!" You know, it is likely that Smith might not have ever had his life turned around or have been saved.

Why Jesus Didn't Quit

This is one of the most powerful principles to learn when you are overcoming any trial or problem. Never quitting was the very thing that made Jesus's ministry so powerful! He didn't quit extending love, faith, forgiveness, and miracles even when they were not always received. He was given every reason to quit, and at one point in His ministry He was sorely tempted to do so.

I mentioned in a previous chapter that Jesus was under such pressure in the Garden of Gethsemane that He began to bleed from His pores while He prayed. I have felt some burdens in my life, but I have never bled from my forehead. That is some serious stress! The Bible says in Luke 22:44 that Jesus was in agony. At this point Jesus wanted to quit because He began to mention it to the Father in prayer, even using the line, "Abba, Father, all things are possible unto thee; take away this cup from me..." (Mark 14:36).

So why didn't Jesus give up under such an immense weight? Most people would want to automatically assume it was because Jesus was the Son of God and, as a result, had greater fortitude than the average human. That is *not* the reason. Jesus was just as Adam was in the garden, and He was given all the same opportunities to fail. I believe there were three major qualities Jesus developed in His life here on Earth that made Him a finisher instead of a quitter.

He made finishing what He started a lifelong quest.

Jesus said it repeatedly. In John 4:34, He said, "My meat is to do the will of him that sent me, and to finish his work." What He meant by the word *meat* was that this quest was the lifelong food that kept Him going. Well, if something is your food, it means you eat of it every day.

Jesus daily "ate" of the revelation that not only did He have a job to do—the will of God—but also that this job was something He was required to finish. He further clarified the Father's will for Himself in John 6:39, when He said, "...all which he hath given me I should lose nothing, but should raise it up again at the last day." Jesus was determined not to lose anything God had given Him.

The way you become a person who finishes is by deciding that, just like Jesus, you will lose nothing that God has given you in His promises. You make the daily decision to get up and get going again, no matter what took place the day before. You decide that you will be a person who finishes what you begin.

He always believed in the power of God.

Jesus was not afraid to say that He was anointed by the Holy Spirit. He believed the presence of God was upon Him all the time. Luke 4:18 says, "The Spirit of the Lord is upon me, because he hath anointed me..." Then Jesus just acted out His daily activities according to that knowledge.

Think how many times we wonder if God is upon us or with us. When things don't quite go the way we want, we tend to think we are facing life all alone. We forget we have been endowed with the power and presence of God. Jesus so expected the power of God to follow Him that He acted out in the miraculous, almost without thought. It takes practice to obtain that kind of faith. But without it we end up giving up on things because we are afraid of failure.

We develop this supernatural kind of faith by talking about it the way Jesus did. The next time you feel defeated and want to quit fighting for your miracle or your deliverance, imagine what would happen if every day you said, "The Spirit of the Lord is upon me because He has anointed me. He has blessed my steps and will grant me a breakthrough in this situation. God's power is working for me right now!" Say that instead of things like, "I don't know how much more I can take!" Do you know what will happen? You will start to believe your words. Think about it: what would happen if, like Jesus, we always believed in the power of God no matter what?

He kept His eyes on the future.

I believe to get Himself through the great trauma of the cross, Jesus had to look beyond His present pain. Think of a time when you went to the doctor's office to get a shot or have a small procedure done, and the doctor or nurse said, "Now this may hurt just a bit." When that happens, you either look away or force your mind to focus on something besides the discomfort you are feeling right then. You have to force yourself to look past the present pain to get through it.

One of the best ways to overcome a present trial is to quit thinking about it so much. Quit calling people on the phone and sharing your painful story or personal frustration over and over again. Jesus had to do that in order to make it through the Crucifixion. Hebrews 12:2 says Jesus endured the cross because He kept His eyes on the joy waiting for Him on the other side. I can just imagine the Lord saying to Himself, "Just wait; in a few days there will be unspeakable joy. The thought of that makes Me so happy."

Jesus couldn't spend hours stewing over what it was going to feel like to have nails driven into His wrists. He couldn't allow Himself to focus on what the weight of all sin was going to do to Him. He knew if He was going to get through it, He had to place His attention on the other side of the cross. People who cannot look past their hurts, frustrations, irritations, or pains will not be people who finish with a miracle. Instead, they will give up on God, themselves, and others.

It Is Finished

Now, as I have mentioned before, I may not enjoy grocery day and the process it takes to clean out the refrigerator at home. The clean-out process, buying food, and restocking the cabinets and freezer are all work. Whenever it is grocery day at our house, however, I always get a refreshed excitement for cooking a good family meal.

A few days prior to grocery day, we find ourselves picking up pizza, stopping at a drive-through, and eating boxed macaroni and cheese. Yet something incredible takes place in me after the food is all put away and there are actually things to cook located in our house. It inspires me.

Even though I'm a little tired from the events of the day, on those nights I have a little more determination than to just serve dinner on paper plates. I want to make it a little more special and light some candles. Then I want to put that extra touch on dinner. You know, those little toppings on the salad you bought, a nice table setting, or a fun dessert for the kids. Suddenly we transform from eating scraps into dining on a meal fit for a king. Everyone in the family always feels just a little different and closer together on these particular days.

There is something that gives you energy when you finish something like that, no matter how large or small. You start to feel good about yourself because you cleaned out the garage, finally got the outside bushes trimmed, organized your office, or cleaned out that closet you once feared opening the door to. And with completion comes new inspiration. Finishing gives you confidence and makes you feel good about yourself. After a day of intense yard work, exhausted and dirty as you are, it feels good to say, "It is finished!"

Having a long list of things you never complete in life will discourage you and give you a negative outlook. Sure, it is sometimes easier to quit working in the yard than to endure the heat and keep going. But at the end of the day, you always come away feeling defeated when you quit.

People who quit things all the time, whether natural or spiritual, go through life with a sense of failure. For some people it is their careers or jobs. They can't seem to find a direction and stay with it. The minute things go badly or they get bored, they are off to find a new job or start another business venture.

Now, that isn't to say that some things in life don't deserve to be abandoned, especially if you realize that your direction has taken you out of the will of God and godly principles. It's the habit of constantly quitting and changing course, however, that will keep you going nowhere. For some people, inconsistency is in regard to their prayer lives, so they struggle to keep themselves in fellowship with God. For others it is as simple as keeping a clean, orderly home. And still some struggle to maintain stable work habits or, most of all, learn how to overcome life's trials by holding on to God with maturity and stability. The ability to look at various things surrounding you and say with confidence, "It is finished," will sustain your life, no matter what the past experience has been. That is what Jesus boldly said while still hanging on the cross.

> When Jesus therefore had received the vinegar, he said, *It is finished*: and he bowed his head, and gave up the ghost.
> —JOHN 19:30, emphasis added

Jesus didn't even allow Himself to die until He was certain that He accomplished everything He was sent to do! Yet notice that He drank some vinegar first. I believe it was a prophetic example that you can finish God's will for your life even when the devil has served up some vinegar.

I can't help but believe that as Jesus was hanging there, although ready to die, He must have had that same sense of accomplishment we feel when we know we completed a task and did a good job. That feeling satisfies you like nothing else can. Yes, maybe you walked through a challenging situation, but to know that you held on to

God's promises with all your might and muscle until you received your breakthrough...

Nothing can match that feeling. It is the feeling of being an overcomer! It feels like diploma day, and, even though we know God rewards our diligence, there is something that happens when you feel that sense of reward deep inside yourself. This time you didn't run from your addiction; you faced it and overcame it. This time you didn't quit school; you got your degree and found a stable job for the long haul. This time you didn't run out of the house, threatening to divorce your spouse, but you stayed in love and controlled your anger.

> To know that you held on to God's promises with all your might and muscle until you received your breakthrough... nothing can match that feeling.

Oh, yes, this time you stood fiercely on God's promise for your healing, and now you are living totally well. No, you didn't revert into another bout of depression when something didn't go your way. Instead, you kept rejoicing in the Lord when you didn't feel like doing so. Perhaps you kept forging through with your parenting skills even though it felt too late and your kids were beyond control. This time you accomplished something; this time you built something for God; this time you didn't throw your hands up in despair. This time you did it, after many attempts, but something supernatural takes place when we finish what we start. Amen to that!

The Finishing Anointing

While finishing things takes determination, we also need God to anoint us supernaturally for the task. Self-determination alone is not enough to win a spiritual war. We need to go beyond just our ability, especially when it comes to our Christian race and personal spiritual growth. Coupled with our own commitment, as I mentioned earlier, we need the power of God to help us. That is why Jesus finished things. Remember? He believed in the power of God to help Him.

> While finishing things takes determination, we also need God to anoint us supernaturally for the task.

As a believer, you have the anointing as Jesus did to finish the work. There is a simple way to make that anointing work in your everyday life no matter what you need to deal with or overcome.

First, Hebrews 12:1–4 holds golden keys for walking in a finishing anointing. Read these verses here carefully, and then make sure you read them again and again in your own Bible. Don't skim or skip over one word of the passage because it will show you how to step into the anointing for finishing. Study each word, meditate on them, and keep them in the forefront of your thinking. Here I want to show the verses to you from The Amplified Bible because this translation literally teaches it to us in one short paragraph. I like to think of this passage of Scripture as vitamins for longevity. You will feel life enter your heart and soul while you read these verses.

> Therefore then, since we are surrounded by so great a cloud of witnesses [who have borne testimony to the Truth], let us strip off and throw aside every encumbrance (unnecessary weight) and that sin which so readily (deftly and cleverly) clings to and entangles us, and let us run with patient endurance and steady and active persistence the appointed course of the race that is set before us, looking away [from all that will distract] to Jesus, Who is the Leader and the Source of our faith [giving the first incentive for our belief]

and is also its Finisher [bringing it to maturity and perfection]. He, for the joy [of obtaining the prize] that was set before Him, endured the cross, despising and ignoring the shame, and is now seated at the right hand of the throne of God.

Just think of Him Who endured from sinners such grievous opposition and bitter hostility against Himself [reckon up and consider it all in comparison with your trials], so that you may not grow weary or exhausted, losing heart and relaxing and fainting in your minds. You have not yet struggled and fought agonizingly against sin, nor have you yet resisted and withstood to the point of pouring out your [own] blood.

Wow! I couldn't have said it better myself. In a few words this passage gives us one power-packed, spiritual vitamin. There are certain keys hidden here that will catapult you into the finishing anointing if you exercise faith for them. I like to think of them as God's twelve-step program to total liberty from the spirit of failure. Each of them is packed with the life of God, and by applying them you will find yourself standing up in power just the way Jesus did.

1. *Know that others have accomplished what you are dealing with.* You are not alone, so don't let the devil isolate you into thinking so.

2. *Throw aside distractions.* Remove the things that keep taking all your time and attention away from your goals.

3. *Separate from sin.* Change where you go, what you watch, and what you say and do. Build new habits and patterns every day.

4. *Run your race, don't walk!* Get excited about finishing a work for God. Don't be lethargic about the things of the Spirit.

5. *Keep your eyes on Jesus and His finishing power.* Jesus is all power, and His presence is resting on your life to accomplish great things.

6. *Keep joy before you.* This means to worship God and rejoice in the Lord daily.

7. *Don't give up, but endure when tested.* Keep rising up again and again, even when you make the same mistakes.

8. *Ignore the pain and shame of the past.* Focus on the future and stop reliving the past.

9. *Remember you are seated with Christ at God's right hand (Eph. 2:6).* God has made you royalty in Christ. Be confident in who you are in Him. You are special!

10. *Compare what Jesus endured against your own trial.* When you take a serious look at what Jesus faced, your situation is probably not as unbearable.

11. *Let Jesus's example encourage you so you don't lose heart.* As you look at the life of Christ, let all He did and who He is wash over your mind and heart.

12. *Realize you have not had to fight the urge to quit until you've bled.* Don't allow the enemy to magnify your problem and make you feel sorry for yourself.

These twelve keys will keep you refreshed, and by thinking on them, you will feel the power of God operating in you. Then as you spend time with God, praying and reading the Bible, the Lord will increase His strength and power on you. Suddenly some things will start happening in your life, and you will rise from failure into power because greater is He who is in you than the enemy who is in the world (1 John 4:4).

Finished in Power and Rewarded With Good

By now you may be realizing that it does not matter what the devil may have tried to do to destroy your purpose or keep you from victory. It really doesn't matter what lie he has screamed into your ear about yourself, your family, or your circumstances. Without a doubt you realize that God is rallying for your breakthrough and has provided every possible way for you to go over the top. To put the icing on the cake, I think it would be in order to go back and look at our dear friends in Ezra and Nehemiah, whom we have ridden along with throughout this book.

> Picture the day when your present problem is only a faint memory. See yourself in the blessing of God.

We have seen how these people of God broke free from the failure of Babylon. Yes, they endured quite a lot, but the best part was that they finished in power. Look at Ezra 6:14, which says, "And the elders of the Jews builded, and they prospered.... And they builded and *finished* it, according to the commandment of the God of Israel..." (emphasis added). I like the way verse 15 says, "And this house was finished."

There is coming a day for you, my friend, when you will look at what the Holy Spirit has built in your life and say, "Wow, we did it, God! You and me, we overcame, and look at how far I have come!" Hold on to that vision and see yourself as a finisher. Picture the day when your present problem is only a faint memory. See yourself in the blessing of God. See the goodness of God all over your life until you just can't picture otherwise.

Our dear friend Nehemiah finished his project on the wall of Jerusalem too. Finally the ugly rubble of Nebuchadnezzar's invasion was nowhere to be found. The stamp Babylon had left on the minds of the people had been replaced by new structures that reflected and pointed to the power and glory of the Lord. Nehemiah 6:15 says, "The wall was *finished*..." (emphasis added). It is almost as if to say, "Take that, devil, right between your eyes because God's work is complete!"

As a result Nehemiah confidently requested something of the Lord (Neh. 5:19) that was very special and intimate, which he repeated again at the end of the book. He said, "Remember me, O my God, for good" (Neh. 13:31). Because of his determined effort and faith, Nehemiah asked the Lord for a reward. Expect God to reward you for rising up out of the things that have invaded your life.

Don't be shy; God wants to do it. He isn't looking to punish you for the past mistakes. God wants you to press for the finish because there is a prize of good at the end of every trying circumstance (Phil. 3:14). God is saying to you today, "Come on, you can do this. I am all you need to propel you into victory. Go ahead; rise up and go with Me! I have a personal blessing on the other side to show you, and it is very good!"

You see, no matter where you have come from or what you have to overcome, God is waiting to bring you out of every personal Babylon and place you on a new road He has decreed. God's hand is upon you as you rise back up to finish your days with power and purpose from a time *when your life has been tampered with*!

Perhaps after reading this book you realize you have never known Jesus Christ in a personal way, and you want an intimate relationship with Him. No matter how much your life has been tampered with, I want to encourage you to begin a new life right now of knowing Him as your personal (your own) Lord and Savior.

Now is the time for you to be free of that Babylonian captivity. My prayer is that you will spend quality time with Him every day. Go ahead and ask Him to fill your heart with His presence and to draw you deeper into a more meaningful relationship with Him. See yourself walking in the blessing of God. Your new life of breakthrough and victory is here!

I want to personally invite you to pray this prayer and receive the promise of eternal life with Him forever!

> *Dear heavenly Father, I dedicate my life from this moment forward to walking in Your victory and freedom. I will pursue You like those I have read about, and I ask You to bless me and my life in the ways You blessed them. In my heart, I truly believe that Your Son, Jesus Christ, died on the cross for me and rose from the dead so I can live forever with You in heaven. You said whoever would call on the name of Jesus would be saved from their sins. I ask You, Jesus, to come into my heart and life. I ask You to forgive me for all my sins. I repent of my wrong-doings, and I commit to live a life that pleases You. Fill me with Your Holy Spirit, and draw me closer to You! From this moment forward, I say I am a Christian, a true lover and follower of Jesus Christ. I desire to know You more than ever before, and today I choose to break free of the captivity of Babylon and finish in Your power! In Jesus's name, amen.*

If your life has been tampered with, remember there is coming a day when you will declare, "Yes, we did it, God! This house is finished!" And friend, let today be that day!

ONE VOICE MINISTRIES
THE MINISTRY OF
HANK & BRENDA KUNNEMAN

CONFERENCES

Hank and Brenda travel worldwide, ministering in churches, conferences, and conventions. They bring relevant biblical messages from a prophetic viewpoint, and their dynamic preaching style is coupled with demonstrations of the Holy Spirit. Though they preach at events separately, they are especially known for their unique platform of ministry together as a team in the ministry of the gifts of the Spirit. For additional information about scheduling a ministry or church conference with either or both of them, contact One Voice Ministries at (402) 896-6692 or request a ministry packet online at www.ovm.org.

BOOKS, PRODUCTS, AND RESOURCES

Books, audio, and video materials are available at the ministry online store at www.ovm.org. Book titles include *When Your Life Has Been Tampered With, Hide and Seek, Don't Leave God Alone*, and *Chaos in the King's Court*. The One Voice Ministries' Web site also provides many ministry resources, including Hank's page called "Prophetic Perspectives" that includes excerpts and prophetic insight on world events. Brenda's page, "The Daily Prophecy," has changed lives around the world. There are also numerous articles for study.

LORD OF HOSTS CHURCH

Hank and Brenda Kunneman also pastor Lord of Hosts Church in Omaha, Nebraska. Filled with captivating praise and worship and sound, prophetic teaching, services at Lord of Hosts Church are always rich with the presence of God. Lord of Hosts Church is known for its solid team of leaders, organized style, and ministry that touches the everyday needs of people. Through the many avenues of ministry the church is raising up strong believers. Many ministries worldwide have referred to Lord of Hosts Church as being one of the most up-and-coming, cutting-edge churches in the United States. For further information about Lord of Hosts Church, call (402) 896-6692, or visit online at www.lohchurch.org or www.ovm.org.

PASTORS HANK AND BRENDA KUNNEMAN
LORD OF HOSTS CHURCH AND ONE VOICE MINISTRIES

5351 S. 139th PLAZA • OMAHA, NE 68137
PHONE (402) 896-6692 • FAX (402) 894-9068
WWW.OVM.ORG • WWW.LOHCHURCH.ORG

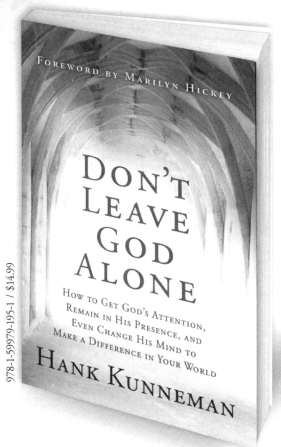